MAKING IT RIGHT

A Common Sense Approach to Criminal Justice

by

Dennis A. Challeen

Illustrations by Patricia Ann Staige

First Edition

MELIUS & PETERSON PUBLISHING CORPORATION

Aberdeen, South Dakota

First Edition
Copyright © 1986 by Dennis A. Challeen

All rights reserved. Printed in the United States of America.

No part of this book may be reproduced or transmitted in any form or by any means, electronic or mechanical, including photocopying, recording or by any information storage and retrieval system now known or to be invented without permission in writing from the publisher, except by a reviewer who wishes to quote brief passages in connection with a review written for inclusion in a magazine, newspaper or broadcast.

Published in the United States by Melius & Peterson Publishing Corporation, Citizens Building, Aberdeen, South Dakota.

Cover Design: Victoria Cavalier
Illustrations: Patricia Ann Staige

Library of Congress Cataloging-in-Publication Data

Challeen, Dennis A., 1936-
    Making it right.

    Includes index.
    1. Sentences (Criminal procedure)—United States.
2. Criminal justice, Administration of—United States.
I. Title.
KF9685.Z9C47 1986   345.73'0772   86-6029
ISBN 0-9610130-7-9   347.305772
ISBN 0-9610130-8-7 (pbk.)

PREFACE

In this book, Judge Dennis Challeen has justly criticized both ends of sentencing and correctional philosophies. The "liberals" rescuing approach of the 1960s, and the present "conservative" punishing approach of today. However, it is not a compromise of the two that he offers; but a significantly different approach ... at least for a large segment of criminals. Responsibility!

He says that the normal, responsible person who sometimes makes a mistake, is "self correcting" and does not need prison to assure that he will never do it again. The Judge is not suggesting any change for the violent offenders (rapists, robbers, murderers, child abusers, etc.). For this ilk, prison is the place. Get them out of society. The same goes for the criminal type he calls the "slick" (alias: the "con man", "sociopath", "psychopathic personality"). While in prison, this "slick" should constantly be confronted with the games he is playing. However, Challeen's "new" (yet, historically old) approach is seen as working best with the greatest portion of prisoners, the irresponsible "slob". The person who continues to commit property offenses, the person with low self-esteem, the person whose continuous behavior guarantees that he does not become a responsible person.

The philosophy expressed in this book is simply stated, thought provoking, and stimulating. It will anger both those who "like punishment" and those who "like to rescue". It calls for a truly radical change in sentencing, whereby a convict is required to negotiate his own sentence (a form of restitution ... sometimes three and four times the lost amount), and be responsible for carrying out the sentence. The authoritarian court has a role change, and the probation officer becomes something else.

These approaches are not just untried theories. They have been tested. In Judge Challeen's analysis, they are working.

>
> Jerome R. Rosonke, PhD.
> Professor of Criminal Justice Studies
> Northern State College
> Aberdeen, South Dakota

TABLE OF CONTENTS

Preface	iii
Introduction	vii
Chapter 1... In The Beginning... Myths	1
Chapter 2... The New Premise	15
Chapter 3... Slicks and Slobs	27
Chapter 4... The Dilemma of the Criminal Justice System	43
Chapter 5... Work, Freeload, Steal or Deal	47
Chapter 6... Restitution	59
Chapter 7... Probation: A Great Idea That Doesn't Work	89
Chapter 8... Solutions	97
Chapter 9... The Little Jimmy Story	125
Afterword	133
Bibliography	
Notes	
Index	

INTRODUCTION

We Americans live in a country with one of the highest crime rates in the world. We also have one of the highest incarceration rates in the world, yet crime continues all around us whether we live in cities, towns or rural areas. Everyone talks about it; and like the weather it seems nobody does much about it. We all seem to have opinions about what "they" should do with "them".

We seem fascinated with crime. Television and the movies portray the criminal as crafty, plotting, shrewd and calculating, yet most crimes are not clever or sophisticated at all. Our images are distorted. We feel we could easily be criminals if we weren't careful and we have little patience with those who cross over the line of legality (unless of course it is one of our children or next of kin, then it becomes poor judgement, a mistake that cries out for understanding). We assume we know what a criminal is, but do we really understand how they think? Psychologists and psychiatrists call chronic criminals character disorders. Much is said about them yet there are very few studies on the "criminal mind". Judges think they know how criminals think, they deal with them every day, but do judges really understand them? Does anyone for that matter? It's obvious criminals do not understand themselves. Most of them are hopelessly caught up in the correction system and can't free themselves from their self-defeating cycles of constant losing.

What is needed is a different viewpoint. It seems in the criminal justice system there are different viewpoints depending upon where one sits. The police officers and prosecutors have their viewpoints, the defense attorney another. The judge has another and the corrections worker yet another, and then there is the criminal who has a whole different perspective.

This book is the product of many hours of discussion between a judge of more than 20 years and an ex-convict who had lived a life of crime for more than 12 years; the judge, trying to make sense out of criminal justice from the vantage point of the bench and the ex-criminal, trying to make sense out of why he was a criminal and what caused him to become rehabilitated.

Criminal justice is a complex subject and this book leaves itself open to criticism of oversimplification. Each page could be expanded greatly, but the text was boiled down to simplistic terms with the intended goal of making a brief readable book that laymen and professionals could both understand. It's often been said that if you can't write an idea on the inside of a matchbook cover you probably don't have a clear idea.

The concepts that hopefully emerge from this book are that our criminal justice system is founded upon a theory that is fundamentally flawed and therefore all that logically follows is doomed for failure; that there are at least three distinct types of criminals who appear before our courts every day and each must be treated totally different; and that the criminal justice system unintentionally makes some criminals worse. And finally, we must create a criminal justice system that promotes individual responsibility rather than useless dependency.

Dennis A. Challeen
Winona, Minnesota
June 1986

Chapter 1

IN THE BEGINNING ... MYTHS

It began in prehistoric times. A Neanderthal man named Errg left his cave to forage food for his family. Errg was a responsible sort...the kind of person who stood on his own two bare feet and worked hard hunting from dawn to dusk so his family could live in caveman comfort. A few caves down the valley lived his neighbor, Glob. Glob was a shifty, lazy, irresponsible, beady-eyed sort who slept a lot and usually freeloaded off the generosity of others. One day Errg was returning home to his cave dragging a small saber-toothed tiger by the tail when he noticed a large hunk of venison he hung up to dry had disappeared. It didn't take much for even the slow mind of a caveman like Errg to conclude that no-good, irresponsible ne'er-do-well Glob had ripped him off again. He picked up his club and stalked straight down the valley to Glob's run-down, dilapidated cave and found the full-bellied Glob smacking and drooling his lips, gnawing on Errg's venison bone. Anger and revenge flooded through Errg's prehistoric mind as he clubbed old Glob over the cranium, knocking him senseless. Errg picked up what was left of his venison bone and ambled on home with a self-satisfied grin on his face. A wrong was made right and thus was the dawn of the criminal justice system.

It hasn't changed much since.

The world spun around the sun millions of times or so since Errg brought justice down upon Glob's head. Through the ages emerged many leaders with enlightened minds as the human race marched, stumbled and slipped through wars, floods, plagues, famines and PCBs. Sometimes sparks of civilization and human potential surfaced in the thoughts and words of the likes of Moses, Jesus, Buddha, Mohammed, Confucius, Franklin, Jefferson, Lincoln, Gandhi and others. The people momentarily listened to them but when push came to shove, mankind always reverted to the great mind and reflex of good old boy Errg and out came the club and we returned to cavemen justice again. Try as we may we just can't get away from that knee jerk solution to crime. An eye for an eye it said in the Old Testament and people have piously quoted that high-minded ideal ever since. Of course Jesus said on the mountain that an eye for an eye was not what justice should be but rather we should turn the other cheek.[1] But people never paid much attention to that. Gandhi said the same thing as Jesus, but he was just a lop-eared, beady-eyed little Hindu, so say the Errgs of today. Thus history marches on and ever so backwards.

Moses of course had some interesting ideas. It seems that when he split out of Egypt after giving the Pharaoh and his gang of cutthroats a bad case of the plague and locust, he wandered around the desert for a spell. His solution to thievery was a direct, uncomplicated scheme. If you stole a sheep, you paid back four sheep.[2] Simple as that. It made you think twice before coveting your neighbor's furry little critters.

It would be interesting to see old Moses as a judge today. Steal your neighbor's Schwinn and you have to buy four bikes in return. Better not eyeball a Rolls Royce or you've got a lifetime of trouble.

Moses' justice was restitution justice, the simplest most honest form of justice there is. Most societies if left alone come up with a restitution type of justice system. The victim is repaid in kind and as a penalty for the crime, the victim is overpaid and the perpetrator not only gives up his ill-begotten gain but forfeits some of his own property to boot. Not a bad system when compared to the nonsense of today.

Take the concept of fines for instance. Back in medieval times if a man stole a sheep from another, he was taken before one of the King's cronies who acted as a magistrate. The sheep farmer was brought in and the magistrate determined how much the farmer lost and ordered compensation...so many shillings, farthings, or coin of the realm. Often three times the loss, so-called treble damages, were paid to the victim of the crime. Well there was nothing wrong with this, just old-fashioned restitution justice hanging around from biblical days. But like anything that is plain common sense, it gets easily corrupted. Along comes the King and he's moaning and groaning that running courts for the sheepherding peasants is a pain in the royal coffers and it is only fair that old number one, the King, should get a cut of the action. So he decides that ten percent of the damages due the victim should be turned over to the King for a little slush fund to keep the court system solvent. He called it a fine. Everyone says that's nice. The peasants of course couldn't grumble too much. They were still coming out ahead. But it soon came to pass as it has with all taxation since the days of Errg and Glob that taxes are easily changed, never downward but always upward. Soon the King was getting half the damages and before long all penalties were forfeited to the Crown, whatever that meant. The fine was extracted from the wrongdoer and paid to His Majesty for disturbing the peace and dignity of his sovereign kingdom...and the sheepherding serf who got ripped off in the first place now got the shaft...nothing new of course.

You would think that revolutions would change things like that but they didn't. When Tom Paine, John Adams, Tom Jefferson and George Washington, et al, told King George to get lost, we should have shucked the justice system with him. But instead we inherited the so-called "Common Law of England" with the adversary system and all its pompous trimmings. Fines continued but went to the sovereign state. And to this very day, American crime victims are oftentimes uncompensated and criminals pay forfeitures to the state, county or city governments for causing a breach of the peace and dignity of the state.

During colonial times, the descendents of Errg reared their ugly heads again. This time they were much more creative. They devised and dreamt up all kinds of devious things to do to the Globs of their times. Instead of whopping them over the heads, they flogged them on the back, branded them with hot irons and mutilated their bodies. This of course made a lot of sense. They took a useless, irresponsible Glob and turned him into a handicapped, useless, irresponsible Glob.

Another curious creation was the stock and pillory. These devices locked the Glob's head and hands in boards attached to a post where the Glob could be held up for public ridicule. We know now of course that criminals have the common denominator of low self-worth covered over and compensated with a cocky, defiant attitude known as "fronting". Fronting masks their low self-worth. The Errgs of those days were no better than the Errgs of today, they reacted to the cocky defiant Globs by "taking them down a notch or two and teaching them smart alecs a lesson they would never forget." Unfortunately it didn't work any better in those days than it does now. The Globs set themselves up to be kicked and the Errgs were more than glad to accommodate them. The end result of the ridicule was to destroy what little self-worth the Globs had, which wasn't much, making matters worse rather than better. However, it kept the Errgs entertained and as ever it gave them the "holier than thou," self-righteous satisfaction of kicking a low-life Glob. When you're down and out, it'll always lift your spirits to know there is always a Glob just around the corner to prove to yourself that you are better than those "shiftless, freeloading, dishonest, untrustworthy, low-life, scum-bag Globs."

The female Globs were branded with the scarlet letter 'A' for adulteress if they happened to be sexually permissive. The man's part in the affair was ignored. But woe be unto the slightly demented female Glob. "Suffer not a witch to live," yelled the pious colonial Errgs, quoting the Bible, and they started their bonfires with some deranged, mentally ill women as a centerpiece.

The European Errgs solved their problem by rounding up all the Globs they could find, gave them a one-way ticket on a ship and sailed them off into the sunset. The Globs landed and settled parts of America. Ironically a lot of them thereafter transformed into Errgs and now you can see them stepping out of pickup trucks with a can of beer in their hand, admiring their shotgun racked up in the rear window. They like to sport-kick Globs...especially Globs of minority races.

The well-intentioned Quakers came along in 1790 and decided with a pang of consciousness that degrading a human, even a miserable Glob, didn't square with what Jesus said on the mountain. So they built the world's first prison on Walnut Street in Philadelphia. The idea was noble enough, they decided to build individual cells and put a Glob in each one with the Bible to read. After a sufficient amount of Bible reading time, by some magic formula, they would let the Glob out and he would repent. Thus was born the word "penitentiary."

Unfortunately Globs don't repent very well, only momentarily, if at all. The Quakers then decided their penitentiaries were not such a good idea after all. But the Errgs who ran them discovered an interesting phenomenon. When you lock up the pesky, useless Globs in cell blocks they are very easy to control. Instead of smart alecky, mouthy, nasty Globs, they turned into docile, passive conforming Globs. A phenomenon that exists to this very day. It was nothing miraculous. We now know that Globs are very dependent and need to be taken care of. Lock a Glob up and he gets comfortable. After all, if deep down, you want to be taken care of, a prison is next to the womb for security. The Errgs didn't know this but Errgs aren't stupid, so they decided that if you're going to put in an eight hour day playing shepherd to a bunch of Globs you might as well have an easy watch. Thus the cell block prison spread all over the world. Not because it rehabilitated the irresponsible lazy Globs, but it made it a heck of a lot easier to control them. Why work any harder than you have to.

Thus was born the prison system.

THE GENESIS OF MYTHS

The anchor man on the local 6 p.m. news looks out into the living rooms of America and with his well-polished voice delivers the most recent violent crime news. Another stabbing, a convenience store was robbed, the clerk was shot, a rape on the campus and another child molested. Night after night the television brings into our homes more and more violence. If it isn't on the news it shows up later as the cops and robbers show. It's in the newspapers, the magazines. It surrounds us, and the little old lady living alone buys another lock for her front door. She vows she will vote for that nice looking politician who says if he is elected he'll crack down on crime and make those criminal coddling lenient judges accountable to the people once and for all.

The truth of the matter is television grossly misrepresents the crime picture in America. Violent crime accounts for about 5% of all crime, yet television reports emphasize the sensational, the stories that jar our innermost fears the most.*

---

* A comparison of violent crime compared to property crime in most states shows that crime is slightly more than 5% violent and 95% property related. The problem is that violent crime is usually reported to law enforcement agencies, while property crime often goes unnoticed. If these factors are taken into consideration, probably 2-3% violent crime would be a more accurate figure.

Television distorts our reality and our response to crime is a direct result of our distorted misconceptions. There is nothing sinister about it. It's simply free enterprise and the news media is a highly competitive business in search of the advertising dollar. Normal crime is boring and a television drama featuring the average street criminal, the Glob who lives down the street, would be a complete bore. Therefore, the script writers pick up on the weird, the creepy, the sinister, the conniving, the shrewd. In reality almost all criminals in the real world who appear in our courts are miserable losers, who have been left behind.

THE JUDICIAL MYTH

In the criminal justice system, the key role is played by the judge. It is the judge who passes sentence upon criminals who appear in the courthouses across America. It is estimated there are about 23,000 judges in America today. Every day they do official acts that send thousands of our fellow citizens off to prison or jails for years of their lives. They uproot families. They destroy relationships. They terminate lives with death sentences. They create welfare. They take children away from their parents, they spend millions of dollars on juvenile treatment programs and contribute to a multitude of suicides.* But do they know what they are doing.

---

* People who are incarcerated commit suicide at a rate 16 times greater than in a city with a population comparable in size to the prison, according to a national study by the National Center on Institutions and Alternatives (NCIA), Washington, D.C.

It has been said that American judges are ill prepared to sentence anyone or do the job they do. Their preparation is law school, to be trained as a lawyer within the adversary system. After sharpening their wits and learning the system, some become judges.* They shift from becoming the advocate to the referee, playing the part they have learned to play. But suddenly they are thrust into the position of determining the destiny of those who are caught up in the system. The problem is law school and the practice of law teach the rules of the game, but once the game is played and it is time to sentence the culprit, the judge finds he is totally lacking in any background in the human behavioral sciences. It is at this point that judges blindly assume they know how to change people's lives, but where and when did they miraculously absorb this insight and wisdom?

There is little or no background in psychology in judge's training. Apparently at the time a lawyer puts on a robe and takes the oath of office to uphold the constitution, something magical happens. A passage occurs. A pronouncement and everyone assumes he now knows how to change people's lives like the Wizard of Oz. The only problem is the storybook Wiz knew he couldn't. Judges believe they can. They simply begin to act like a judge is supposed to act. Since they have practiced before many judges, they have a multitude of role models to choose from, and so the myth perpetuates itself.

There is very little original thinking when it comes to sentencing. Law is a profession of studying precedent—looking backward for the answers.

---

* In many European countries judges are trained and follow a different course of education from those who become attorneys. In America there are Judge's Colleges like the National Judicial College, University of Nevada-Reno. Unfortunately, as their faculty and staff will confirm, the judges who need the training the most attend the least.

THE LENIENCY MYTH

In the coffee shops across the country, in the taverns on the corners, it is said over and over again. "Those darn judges are too lenient." The newspaper editorial says it as an undisputed fact and the syndicated columnists repeat it. It's assumed without question that judges are too soft. But it's another American myth. American judges are the toughest in the world.[3] On a per capita basis the U.S. incarceration rate is one of the highest in the industrialized world. Only Russia and South Africa consistently lock up more of its citizens than we do.

The Russians imprison political dissidents and people who make anti-Soviet remarks. The South Africans jail blacks who run afoul of racial apartheid law. None of these violations would be crimes in America. If you subtract these "artifical" offenses, we probably live in the toughest, most lock-em-up happy country in the so-called free world. Yet our crime rate is one of the highest in the world.

On a per capita basis, we incarcerate twice as many people as Canada, three times as many as Great Britain and four times as many as West Germany.[4]

During the entire decade from 1963 to 1973 the Dutch sentenced only two persons to life imprisonment. Florida, with only half the population of the Netherlands, sentenced more than 2,000 human beings to life imprisonment.[5]

The American judge is not lenient, the people simply have nothing to compare them with and conclude erroneously that our judges are soft. It's just another myth.

THE REVOLVING DOOR MYTH

Almost everyone has heard it. "Those darn parole boards. They let out criminals too early, before their time is up, before they have learned their lesson." Another myth. The median time of incarceration in the U.S. is 21 months. By comparison, Sweden is 3 months and Holland less than a month.[6]

One of the major factors that contribute to our overcrowded jails and prisons are the extremely long term sentences that are routinely handed out by our tougher than the rest of the world judges. Long-term sentences are necessary for violent offenders. Not because it will rehabilitate them, but to protect society. Murderers, rapists, child molesters and brutal people must be locked up, they have forfeited their right to be free, society must be made safe from them, but these types of people make up a small part of the criminal population in America. Less than 5% of the criminal population, and a minor portion of the prison population. The problem is our prisons are filled to the brim with life's losers, the left behinds—people who cannot survive in the normal game of life. Our modern day Globs. Irresponsible people who won't take charge of their lives, own their problems or direct themselves in a positive, constructive way. The problem is when you lock up a lagging behind irresponsible loser for two years, what comes out is a lagging behind irresponsible loser who is now two more years behind.

THE PRISON CURE MYTH

Many Americans believe that convicting criminals and locking them up equals justice, that it is now up to the corrections system to "correct" them. Some legislators (a collection of realtors, lawyers, insurance agents, school teachers, housewives, etc.) go so far as to prescribe the exact length of time necessary to cure them, and when it doesn't work, like any recipe, they add a little more time. Another myth. A study of crime rates and length of incarceration among our states reveal no relationship whatsoever. Some states have a high incarceration rate and a high crime rate while others have a low crime rate and a low incarceration rate. Others defy both extremes and have a high incarceration rate with a low crime rate or vice versa. It seems some states simply choose to waste more money than others with no proof that it affects their crime rate whatsoever. Most crime experts conclude that locking up people has no relationship to crime rates. Crime has its roots in sociological and psychological factors unrelated to what we do with criminals after we catch them. Like locking up the barn after the cows are out, it's anticlimactic. A fire chief can have a wonderful record of putting out house fires but that has nothing to do with future fires. Fires are usually caused by human carelessness. Crime has its genesis at the kitchen table and it doesn't make a bit of difference to the fledgling criminal that there is a penetentiary full of has-been criminals just down the road. Out of sight and out of mind.

THE "GET THEM OFF THE STREET MYTH"

Prosecutors often submit to judges that even if prisons don't rehabilitate (most of them concede this point) it is a victory for society to get them off the streets so they can no longer prey on society. This is a simplistic argument that most people buy at first glance. It definitely applies to vicious, violent and depraved criminals. No one can argue with that proposition. However when you apply it to the 95% of losers who are locked up for property crimes the argument is not so simple. The theory would be true if the offender "got better" but if the government is simply spending tax money to make them worse then we are the fools. It is now clear that prison life brings out the worst in losers. Putting them in an unreal world where everyone is warped cannot "straighten out" anyone. If any American was picked up and dropped into a totally alien environment and culture, such as China, and they had to remain in China with only Chinese for company, it would not take too long before one would become Chinese. A person would soon speak their language out of necessity. In short one would become culturally like them. Humans are remarkably adaptable to the world they must deal with. Only a fool would submit that one lone American would change the multitude of Chinese around him. The same principle applies to prisons. The new inmate adapts and becomes part of the prison culture. Very few can do their time and walk away unchanged or unabsorbed by this environment. Further, the cost is outrageous. We as a society will take a $100.00 burglar and put him away for years at a cost of $20,000.00 or more a year in a College of Criminal Knowledge and wonder why the system doesn't work. We can take a kid (most criminals are between 16 and 25 years of age) and spend thousands of dollars a year on him to make him a worthless dependent when we can give him a college education for four years for the cost of one year of incarceration.*

Our county or city jails are no better. We now know that we can lock up an offender in the Holiday Inn and eat off the menu for a lot less than we can house them at the local jail.

Of course locking up a loser in the Holiday Inn would not be justice to the average person. Incarceration to be effective must make the prisoner miserable otherwise there is no justice so the logic goes. Those who subscribe to this theory might be surprised at the actions of one Minnesota sheriff.

It seems the state condemned the county jail before a bond issue for a new jail was submitted to the voters. They soon found locking them up in a motel was cheaper than running a jail. The embarrassing part of it all was no one tried to escape.[7]

Of course Minnesota is unusual in many respects. It consistently has one of the lowest incarceration rates per capita in the nation yet one of the lower crime rates in America. The state has sentencing guidelines that mandate locking up violent criminals but forbids judges to incarcerate property criminals unless they accumulate enough points after multiple offenses. The aim is to keep the prison population at a minimum. Ironically, the state of Wisconsin next door believes in locking up their losers to a maximum, so their prisons are overflowing and Minnesota "rents out" vacant cell blocks to their Wisconsin neighbors at more than $20,000.00 per year per inmate. The business of making people worthless can be profitable.

---

* A New Mexico judge tried to do just exactly that. He sentenced a woman to go to college for four years or go to prison for the same period of time. This common sense conservative judge was criticized. The prosecutor threatened to quit. After all, justice in America is punishment and punishment equals justice regardless of the cost. Whatever happened to saving money and the old work ethic of being a useful citizen anyway.

THE STREET CRIMINAL MYTH

The average person when confronted with the mental image of a criminal usually thinks of a shadowy, mean, menacing figure of a bandit in dark clothes creeping around in the shadows doing crimes to victims who are strangers to him. The typical TV image of a street criminal comes immediately to mind. However, the real criminal in America doesn't fit that image at all, he is the opposite in all respects. In terms of money and sheer number of crimes the white collar criminal rips everyone off by at least 10 to 1 and maybe as high as 16 to 1 over the street criminal. The modern smooth looking man in a three piece suit and a briefcase is by far a greater threat to your financial security than some loser who rips off a cigarette machine to get him through another day of his useless miserable life. Yet who do we fear the most—the street criminal because he is much more alien to us. Which brings us to another myth. Crime statistics clearly reveal that if we are a crime victim more often than not the perpetrator will be someone we know rather than a stranger. The most dangerous people are our next of kin, our friends and relatives. Far down the list is the stranger who attacks us, but they are feared the most.

OUR UPSIDE DOWN PRISONS

If prisons were filled proportionately according to crime in America, they would be filled with white collar criminals and about one out of ten would be a street loser. There would be a lot of child molesters and tax cheaters (the justice system only touches the tip of the iceberg for these crimes) and they would be white and average American in most all respects. But what we find in our overcrowded prisons and jails is exactly opposite. Blacks are imprisoned at a rate 8½ times that of whites and receive more severe sentences.[8] Also, the average inmate is handicapped physically and educationally and they are life's losers who are caught up in a self-defeating merry-go-round that they cannot comprehend or escape. They are multiple time losers who have been in and out of one correction center or another. Many are there because they violate correction department rules rather than commit new crimes...people who cannot function in a normal free society without self-destructing and hurting others in the process. They are life's losers who sit and stagnate and with every day they become further behind and less able to ever catch up. And we spend millions of tax dollars to continue the senseless waste of human worth. Out of sight, out of mind. Yet even those who are concerned are at odds about the solution. Perhaps the premises are wrong. According to the principles of logic, if the premises are wrong, the conclusion will be wrong. What is necessary is new premise...

Chapter 2

THE NEW PREMISE

There are many well meaning legislators who believe you can pass a law and solve a problem. Since criminals are universally disliked, they can become easy targets for the ambitious lawmaker. There is not much you can say on behalf of crime, therefore everyone steps aside and allows politicians to make political hay against this evil. Their motives are to make a safer society. Unfortunately they are uninformed and ill advised in their conclusions. They generally make one fatal premise and that is the conclusion that criminals think like legislators or supreme court judges or other responsible members of our society—"what would work on me will work on them." This premise often leads to failure in view of what we now know about criminal mentality today.

THE STORY OF EDITH

Edith is a lady in her sixties, she is a well respected lady of the community. She belongs to the ladies bridge club and volunteers a good deal of her time to charity. Her home is immaculate and her yard and garden are well trimmed. A punctual person, she lives a well organized life. She is the treasurer of her church and has served on various committees whenever called upon to serve. She learned to drive an automobile when she was 20 and was never involved in a traffic mishap. Her insurance rating is tops. One day

Edith had her mind on her responsibilities and she drove straight through a stop sign and was arrested by a police officer who narrowly missed colliding with her. Edith appeared the next day in court. She hadn't slept a wink the night before and was emotionally distraught when the judge asked her how she pled. "Guilty," she squeaked, with tears welling up in her eyes.

"I'm so sorry this happened," said Edith, "I'm going to sell my car. I could have killed someone or myself...I don't know how this happened."

The judge, looking over her traffic record replied, "You have a perfect record for a driver. I think selling your car would be rather drastic. Under the circumstances it appears to be a human mistake you don't normally make. We all make mistakes."

"Will my name be in the records or in the newspaper?" sobbed Edith. The judge told her not to worry about that. "What will the ladies down at the bridge club say when they hear about this, I'm so embarassed."

"Oh, I think you are overreacting, certainly they are understanding," replied the judge.

"It's so embarassing and I could have hurt myself or run over some small child. I just would never forgive myself if that happened. I'm going to sell my car," says Edith.

"Don't do that, I'll tell you what I'll do. Since you have a perfect record I will suspend your fine," said the judge.

Well, Edith left the courtroom and sold her car. There was no way she was ever going to get herself in a jam like this...ever again.

On a responsibility scale of one to ten, Edith is a ten. She does not allow herself to make errors and will take whatever steps are necessary to remove the small amounts of risk that may crop up in her life.

THE STORY OF ERNIE

Ernie is a 60-year-old man who never held down a steady job all his life. He's an alcoholic and lives day to day. He lives on handouts and gets a meal now and then when he sweeps out a bar in the morning. He gets some food stamps and plays a harmonica around the tavern for the free beers he gets from some patrons. When things get tough, Ernie gets sticky fingers and shoplifts something to eat or to sell for more liquor. Every once in a while he gets caught and appears in court. Ernie is a familiar sight to the judge.

"Good morning, Ernie."
"Good morning, Judge."
"It says here you've been charged with theft again."
"Yup."
"How do you plead?"
"Guilty."
"What did you steal this time?"
"A flashlight."
"Why?"
"Buy booze."

The judge has heard the same story with little variation for years. Ernie has been committed to alcohol treatment programs numerous times. He's not interested. Ernie is a miserable person but not miserable enough to change. The judge has tried everything from long jail sentences to AA, psychological evaluations to support groups and back to anabuse. Nothing works.

You see, Ernie is a loser and doesn't want to help himself. On a responsibility scale of 1 to 10, Ernie is a zero.

The two stories illustrate the differences there are among people in our society. Edith is responsible to an extreme, she over controls her life while Ernie is irresponsible to an extreme. He does nothing to help himself. Between Edith and Ernie, the two far extremes, is the rest of the population.

People like Edith are in charge of their lives. They own their problems and are responsible. When they make errors of judgement they immediately take charge of the problem and correct it. They run their own ship. To penalize Edith is unnecessary, she corrects her own course and eliminates the problem and takes steps to make sure it doesn't happen again.

Ernie on the other hand is a loser who views life as bad luck or "they're picking on me again." If he gets caught stealing, the worst that can happen to him is jail and to Ernie that's not bad at all. He's unconcerned about his reputation, he's in control of his life at a bare minimum only enough to get him through another day. Ernie doesn't want to own his problems and it doesn't matter what a judge does to him. As long as he doesn't want to change, there is little if anything a judge can do to change him.

To carry this logic to its conclusion it can be argued that it doesn't matter what the judges sentence people to. The Ediths or the responsible people of our society correct themselves and the Ernies and the irresponsible people of our society are unaffected because they choose not to change and simply endure whatever is given them. This conclusion is hard on judge's and lawmaker's egos. But let's pursue this proposition further. If there were no consequences many people on the borders of self-control and responsibility would easily cross over the line and commit crime with impunity. Therefore we need consequences as a deterrent so we know consequences will be imposed when we commit unlawful acts. However, society seems to blindly assume that all consequences must be punishment in nature. Jail and prison seem to be the automatic consequence. Often the consequences that naturally flow from our wrongdoings are sufficient in themselves. A person who fails to yield to a train and ends up in a hospital doesn't need a judge to tell him trains are dangerous. An employee who steals on the job and is fired doesn't need a judge to tell him about the price of dishonesty. A lawyer who is disbarred loses his livelihood. A banker who embezzles loses his job and usually must pay back what he has stolen. Nevertheless, consequences need not be negative or degrading in nature. Yet our knee jerk answer to crime is usually to degrade, incarcerate and exile.

If we accept the fact that murderers, rapists, armed robbers, child molesters and those who commit acts of brutal violence on others should be locked up to protect society (less than 5% of all crime) our prisons and jails would be virtually empty. Our problem is that we clog our corrections system with losers, people who we don't rehabilitate but who in fact are made worse at an enormous cost to taxpayers both in money and loss of human productivity.

The rest of this book focuses on this problem.

THE JUDGE WHO GOES TO PRISON

A judge one day after hearing a prosecutor demand incarceration for the guilty defendant challenged the prosecutor to spend some time in jail or prison and experience firsthand the wonderful curative results of incarceration. The prosecutor being busy refused, the judge however contacted the commissioner of corrections and was allowed to enter the prison as an inmate for three days.* With a certain apprehension, the judge entered prison and lived the life of an inmate for 72 hours of his life. After sleeping in a locked cell and going through the chow line with the convicts and living the life of society's throw aways, the judge emerged relieved but glad he made the effort. His conclusion was he had witnessed a waste of human life and dignity. He also concluded that he would absolutely never commit a crime that would ever result in having to spend a great deal of time in a prison. The judge knew however that a great share of the inmates who leave prison quickly resume their life of crime and return to prison again and again. The judge then concluded:

Punishment deters a major part of society ... the part that is not the problem.

---

* Editor's Note: The judge who voluntarily experienced three days of education in jail is the author of this book.

THE RESULT OF PUNISHMENT ON WINNERS & LOSERS

REASONS FOR SUCCESS
1. Good self-worth
2. Knows what responsibility is
3. Learns from mistakes
4. Owns & deals with the problem
5. Concerned about reputation
6. Good probability estimation
7. Refuses to accept failure

Positive effect

REASONS FOR FAILURE
1. Negative-low self worth
2. Avoids responsibility
3. Blames others
4. Repeats mistakes
5. Believes in "bad luck"
6. Refuses to own or deal with the problem
7. Poor probability estimation

Negative effect

Successful people oftentimes have little patience for losers...especially dishonest losers. "I made it. Why can't he get off his dead rear end and get going."

The problem is there is a great deal of difference between winners and losers and the differences are not readily visible. Since all average people, except the handicapped or retarded, start out relatively even, it would seem that we all have an equal chance to be successful and none of us have to end up being a criminal. To the winner it seems as if it's a conscious choice, but is it really a conscious choice? Somewhere along the line, somewhere among the millions of events that shaped our childhood and adolescence and young adulthood, some of us learned responsibility and some of us didn't. Some of us turned out winners and some of us ended up losers, some of us a little of both. Some of us can point to exact events or people who by their examples helped shape our lives. Some of us never had anyone.

WINNER	LOSER
Independent	Avoids being responsible
Authentic	Manipulative
Credible	Without purpose
Responsible	Build their own cages
Reveal themselves rather than image	Doesn't live in present
	Bemoans bad luck
Loving rather than acting loving	Shifts responsibility to others
	Blames others
Self-confident	"If only"
Think for themselves	Waits to be rescued
Don't play helpless or blaming games	Pessimistic about future
	Anxiety over the present
Respond to situation	Play-acting and pretending
Live here and now	Maintain mask and phoney front
Spontaneous	Afraid to try new things
Adaptable	Maintain status quo
Zest for life	Afraid to try new things
Enjoy accomplishments	Repeat their own mistakes
Enjoy accomplishments of others	Is not intimate, direct or honest
	Rationalize and excuse-making
Seek goals in appropriate ways	Potential remains dormant[1]
Cares about the world and people	
Concerned about quality of life	
Makes the world a better place	

The average reasonably intuitive judge, if asked to sit down and list the characteristics of those who regularly appear before his court, could easily list ten or more negative points that uniformly manifest themselves in chronic losers. Psychologists label them character disorders, but in the lexicon of the criminal justice system they become known as losers, a handle for a person who can't get his or her life together. Losers are people who live at the expense of others. They constantly defeat themselves and by their losing acts, cause the establishment to come down on them, and as we shall see, contribute to their losing ways.

COMMON CHARACTERISTICS OF LOSERS IN THE CRIMINAL JUSTICE SYSTEM

1. Anger, low self-esteem
2. Anti-authoritarian
3. Irresponsible
4. Quits easily
5. Blames others
6. Lies, cheats and manipulates
7. Fronts with arrogant behavior
8. No priority system
9. No guilt feeling
10. Fails to learn from mistakes
11. Alienated from community
12. Not loyal or trustworthy
13. Gravitates to negative friends
14. Exploits those good to him
15. Accepts and expects failure
16. Alcohol and drug dependency

THE PROFILE OF A LOSER

1. ## Anger, Low Self-Worth
   All pre-sentence reports usually start out this way.
2. ## Anti-Authoritarian
   Losers constantly are at odds with authoritarians.
3. ## Irresponsible
   They avoid being responsible to themselves or other persons.
4. ## Quits Easily
   A loser is easily discouraged.
5. ## Blames Others
   A winner says "I fell"; a loser says "Who pushed me."
6. ## Lies, Cheats and Manipulates
   When you are irresponsible, authorities enter your life and your choices are to admit responsibility or to try and get out of it.
7. ## Fronts With Arrogant Behavior
   Fronting is a mask to cover up fear, inadequacy and low self-worth.
8. ## No Priority System
   Losers have never experienced achievements, therefore long range goals are unrealistic to them.
9. ## No Guilt Feelings
   When you can't like yourself and are angry toward the world, you don't care if anyone else is hurt.
10. ## Fails To Learn From Past Mistakes
    Winners take charge of their lives. Losers blame bad luck and say people are picking on them.
11. ## Alienated From The Community
    People who are not very nice are usually avoided in the community.
12. ## Not Loyal Or Trustworthy
    Losers are parasites who use other people to survive—friends, relatives, employers are the easiest to exploit.
13. ## Gravitate To Negative Friends
    People usually choose friends who think and feel as they do.

14. Exploits Those Good To Him
They are the easiest to exploit.

15. Accepts And Expects Failure
When your life has been a continuous losing streak, there is little reason to expect otherwise.

16. Alcohol And Drug Dependent
"The only time I feel good about myself is when I'm drunk."

Chapter 3

SLICKS AND SLOBS

The foregoing criteria for losers is obviously oversimplified, but closer observation of the character disorder reveals that they break down into two general types. There may be more, but judges and corrections workers see these two types surface the most. They are arbitrarily labeled "The Slick" and "The Slob". Their personality characteristics will be described in masculine terms but the same applies to women.

THE SLICK

A Slick is an Errg who has gone crooked or always was crooked. There are a lot of Slicks out in this world and they commit many crimes but judges rarely get to sentence them because they are rarely caught. If they are caught they are hard to convict. Lawyers like to defend them because they don't confess and have a planned defense in the event they are caught. They've been around a lot and they are your professional criminal. Streetwise and clever, they usually avoid apprehension unless they get careless or try to push a good thing too far. A Slick wasn't born slick but he was born with above normal intelligence. As a child he just didn't get along and was either abused physically or in his mind treated unfairly or discounted by those in control. He soon developed an attitude that "I'm all right but you certainly are not". He then quickly perceives that the adult world is full of inconsistencies, that rules are arbitrarily applied and that if you are smart you can get around just about anything. Since there is an element of truth in his perception he soon decides he's as smart as all the people who are considered smart. His parents, the teachers, the principal, the cops, the prosecutor, the probation officer, the judge, the prison guard, etc. But he is a shortcutter. He doesn't want to go about acquiring wealth and position by the old-fashioned way of "earning it". He's too impatient and according to his own conclusion "he's smarter than them already". He becomes addicted to the game of "I'm smarter than you" and his whole life revolves around constantly proving to himself that he is. That's his payoff. It proves "I'm OK but you're not". Slicks love to play "let's make a fool out of you" and "NIGYSOB"[1], which is short for "now I got you, you son of a bitch". Everyone who has ever played a game and was victorious knows the feeling. In chess it's the feeling one gets after an hour or two of mental combat on a chessboard, you reach over and make a final move and you sit back with a smile and say "checkmate" (or now I got you, you son of a bitch).

Slicks are clever and manipulative. They use people and the people never know they have been used until it's too late. They are leaders and trusting people follow them. They are loners because they trust no one, in fact they shy away from any intimate relationships or friendships because their life since childhood has taught them that to get involved with someone only leads to hurt and the danger of being ripped off emotionally. Their relationships are superficial. They are masters at trapping the other side into becoming emotionally involved with them because it feeds their ego. But it is only a one-sided relationship where it is only a matter of time before they get dumped. Women who fall in love with a Slick will soon become a miserable puppet with the Slick totally in control. Many women have wound up in prison because they are taking the rap or were set up by their "true love", a Slick.

Slicks operate out of their "Little Professor", that part of us that schemes, plots and manipulates to get what we want. Only Slicks have a "Little Professor" with a Doctor's Degree, a highly developed part of their personality that works overtime to obtain what the Slick wants by shortcutting and getting the best of their trusting victims. The movie *"The Sting"* was a prime example of Slicks out-slicking Slicks. We loved it and completely overlooked the total immorality of what the movie portrayed. J. R. Ewing is a Master Slick.

Slicks are driven by anger, they just don't like society in general and their controlled anger is vented and satisfied by making a fool out of you, the victim. "You should have seen the dumb look on his face when he found out he had been taken." "I would have loved to hear what they said when they discovered all their money was missing." They love the game of putting you in a "no win"

The Slick

position because it proves in their mind that "I'm smarter than you." They crave excitement and crime is their outlet to obtain the excitement.

A Slick doesn't know what guilt feelings or remorse are. If your life stance is "I'm OK, you're not", the victim's emotions are simply "tough luck sucker".

A judge who is impressed with a defendant showing great remorse is either being fed an act or he doesn't have a Slick in front of him.

Remorse is an emotion a Slick just doesn't have. He knows what it is by watching others but he doesn't feel it because it runs contrary to his basic premise that "I'm all right, you're not."

Slicks are strong believers that others must play by the rules since he has concluded those who set the rules must believe in their rules and abide by them. Since he never agreed to follow the rules and has no respect for rules, he doesn't abide by the rules. But the establishment must abide by the rules because the rules are a framework that he operates within as long as the rules are to his advantage. He becomes very angry when policemen violate his constitutional rights when he may have just violated another person's total rights and dignity as a human being. When the cops don't play by the rules or the judge doesn't back him up in his claim it reinforces his belief that you're "just as rotten as I am, so don't try to preach to me". He glories in righteous indignation.

A Slick admires lawyers because in his mind lawyers know how to use rules against the very society that created the rules. He is fascinated by courtroom drama and sees it as another way to "make a fool out of you." When you lock up a Slick he goes directly to the law library and becomes a jailhouse lawyer.

When you imprison a Slick he looks at his incarceration as "bad luck" and immediately plans how to manipulate himself out. Society may have momentarily won but "he'll come out on top, you wait and see". Thus the game never ends.

By the way, not all Slicks are crooks. Slicks are sprinkled throughout society. Being a Slick in the business world is acceptable as long as you stay on the right side of the law. Slicks often become lawyers or politicians and as long as they don't cross over the ethical or legal barrier, they will be successful. Slicks who end up in prison don't give a damn about law, ethics or morality.

When Slicks are arrested they hire their own lawyers and if they need money to bond out, they arrange it. They simply pay for it by committing more crime.

If a Slick is going to use drugs it will be a stimulant. A Slick shuns alcohol because it makes him dull and a Slick always likes to keep his mind razor sharp.

REHABILITATION OF SLICKS

Since the dominant game of a Slick's life is to prove "I'm smarter than you", he gambles with the establishment every time he commits a crime. He likes con games, fraudulent get rich quick schemes, easy come easy go. He realizes that he gambles prison every day and is willing to throw the dice. It's the price of the game if he gets caught. But even when he is caught he figures the game is not up, that he's smart enough to beat the rap if he and his lawyer can out "chess game" the prosecutor, judge and jury. Once in prison he will play the rehabilitation game to the max. If a drug treatment program will look good, he'll play the drug addict. If religious conversion would look nice, he'll fake a religious conversion. He will befriend the prison staff if he can manipulate himself out. The game doesn't cease just because he's locked up. He loves drama and will sow the seeds of a prison riot, playing inmate against inmate, or inmate against the guards. He loves to play "Lets you and him fight." He'll sell information for an early release and on and on until he hits the streets, then it's back to the game of crime all over again.

Slicks should be locked up along with violent people simply to protect society, but that's no solution.

Rehabilitation of a Slick starts the day he realizes the game his life is caught up in. That he's winning at losing, he's on a perpetual merry-go-round to nowhere. That if he's so damn smart why is he in prison and the "saps" he's ripped off are not. Once he comes to this realization he can change. But change must come from within himself. A judge can't change a Slick but a Slick can change himself. A Slick must be challenged to aim his energy in a legitimate way, the world is full of legitimate Slicks who are making fortunes and are successful every day. Legitimate Slicks play the same games of "I'm smarter than you", "NIGYSOB" and "I'll make a fool out of you." Many salesmen knock on the door of a prospective customer with the same games in mind as any Slick. What a dishonest Slick must do is become a legitimate Slick and that's not easy. Make a car dealer out of him, make him a sales manager, a realtor, a promoter or public relations practitioner, but whatever you do, make sure he's not in charge of the checkbook and have him monitored by a trustworthy, legitimate Slick because it takes one to know one. Slicks can be rehabilitated and they often are but they will walk the narrow line between legality and illegality for the rest of their lives.

Slicks cause a lot of crime in America. If you incapacitate one you stop a lot of crime. However the criminal justice system sees very few of them and when they are caught they usually slip away with plea bargains and other maneuvers. Nevertheless, if we locked up all the crooked Slicks in the country, our prisons would be relatively empty.

The overcrowded prison population in America is not the result of locking up violent people or Slicks. Our problem is the next overwhelming group of character disorders who clog our system. We call that group the Slobs.

THE SLOB

A Slob is a Glob who has gone crooked. They're all over the place. They clog our courts, jails and consume our tax dollars in outrageous amounts. They bring our justice system to a grinding halt.

A Slob is the opposite of a Slick in all respects except they are both a parasite on society.

A Slob has low self-worth and feels useless. He has a life position of "I'm not OK but you're all right I suppose". He was born with the same tools as everyone else but somewhere in his childhood at the kitchen table or elsewhere he was told he was not OK and he believed it. He didn't arrive at that conclusion all by himself. Usually there is a dominant negative parent or a parent who ignores the child or a marshmallow for the other parent if there is any. He's caught between parents and never learns responsibility. If you tell a kid he's no good often enough, sooner or later he'll believe it. He lacks self-confidence and when he goofs up, it's only evidence that confirms the fact he is no good. He never learned responsibility because he was either stifled by the dominant parent and was overprotected, nurtured and coddled by a marshmallow parent. By the time he hits school he has determined that he's inadequate and when the school system gets through with him he'll be certified in black on white records to prove he's a loser, complete with label and all.

A Slob never acquires the fundamental concepts of self-worth and responsibility. Consequently he develops a dependent personality. He needs someone to be responsible for him and wants another person to make decisions for him. To make decisions for himself and to be responsible is stress that he draws away from. He discovered at an early age that if you do nothing there is a world full of rescuers. People who feel good when they can help a helpless Slob out of a stressful situation. Slobs soon learn to play "stupid" then someone will suggest the solution, stroking a rescuer's ego so they will take over the problem. If the solution doesn't work then the Slob can always blame them for it. It was your idea and the rescuer can walk away feeling guilty. They learn to cope with failing to be responsible by being defiant ("Quit picking on me"—"get off my back" or "go to hell"). The other method is to adapt and become a pawn of the authoritarian. This is accomplished by bootlicking, playing fencepost (non-communicative—looking at the floor, doing nothing like a fence post). A Slob subconsciously doesn't want to own his problems or be responsible, in fact he avoids responsibility by using all kinds of techniques. During his school years he displayed a passive, don't give a damn attitude towards education in spite of all the rescuer's efforts. Once he burns out the rescuers, he's adrift...alienated from the rest of his age peers. He likes to do as he pleases as long as someone else will support him. If he loses his support system, he by necessity must turn to crime. It's turn to crime or become employed. Employment requires responsibility and self-discipline. Employers require them to be on the job, to think for themselves, to take over the problem, to be responsible for their assigned duties, to be reliable. These are characteristics that are repugnant and stressful to a Slob—so he blows it by absenteeism, getting drunk, being defiant to the foreman, stealing on the job or by being inadequate and irresponsible. He gets fired and loses again and blames others for it.

Slobs are symbiotic. They need a support system. They don't function as a self-directed, independent, responsible person, instead they must be carried or lean on others. In life there are four options for everyone. We can work, freeload, steal or deal. There are no other options. Since a Slob has a difficult time making it in the workforce he must freeload. If he cannot find another person to support him he has no other alternative other than crime. Either stealing or dealing are his only options.

The problem is Slobs make lousy criminals. Their crimes are impulsive, stupid and without much planning. Slicks shrewdly plan crimes, Slobs stumble in. Slicks get away with crime, Slobs usually get caught. Deep down they want to get caught because the worst that can happen to them is society will take over their life and they no longer have to be responsible. Our jails and prisons are the ultimate in taking over a person's life. They become totally dependent on the state and, sure, they lose their freedom but to a Slob freedom isn't what it is to the average responsible person. Freedom means responsibility and remember Slobs don't like responsibility. They love to be free without responsibilities but the world doesn't work that way. To be free you must also be self-sufficient. You can't have one without the other unless you can find someone to freeload off—someone to take over your responsibilities.

Slobs learn from early on that when you screw up in this world it attracts attention. Two types of people arrive on the scene—the kickers or rescuers. The kickers are in the form of the police, prosecutor, the judge and corrections workers—the rescuers come in the form of social workers, defense attorneys, probation officers, counselors, friends and relatives. Whoever wins control in the end is of little consequence because the Slob gets taken care of either way. He ends up in prison (the ultimate welfare state) or he gets rescued and escapes responsibility by those who take over his problem for him. In the end he gets taken care of.

Judges and probation officers are often amazed when a criminal who has been down and out finds steady employment, gets a promotion then self-destructs by doing some dumb, impulsive, irresponsible act. "He had it made and then he blows it all", cries

The Slob

the probation officer. The trouble is that Slobs can't stand success. Employment requires responsibility, promotions require more responsibility and Slobs can't stand responsibility and subconsciously the Slob always knows that when you mess up, responsibility will be taken from you.

Slobs usually find a niche in this world, either a job with the minimum of responsibility that tolerates their occasional irresponsibility or they can find a responsible or semi-responsible person to glob onto. Often this is in the form of a strong wife or husband who will take over the responsibilities, pay the bills, make the important decisions and carry the weight. This of course gets the Slob rescued and in a stable condition. Slobs like this but it also brings on another of their character traits. A Slob is very jealous and possessive. He is symbiotic in nature...like a parasite needs a host. He is insecure and closely looks out for any threat to his security. The problem is that he feels put down by being in the inferior position of being taken care of and when under stress, or the influence of alcohol, he feels he must rebel. This is the type of person judges see on a Monday morning after the Slob gets drunk, tells off his wife or beats her up. He sits repentant, asks for forgiveness and promises "it will never happen again". Slobs are good at momentary repentance. And women who marry Slobs are good at believeing them. People in sick symbiotic relationships need each other and so the drama continues for another day.

Slobs are often depressed, they feel failure but seem to be helpless in doing anything about it. Slobs drift into alcoholism easily. When they are drunk they can be somebody, however, they usually commit their crimes when they are drunk also. That's why Slobs are so easy to catch. Any mystery writer or script writer for a movie or TV show would never write a story about crimes committed by a Slob. It would be boring, mundane and without a plot. Their crimes are easily solved because the perpetrator really doesn't give a damn if he gets caught or not. If he gets away with it, he survives for another day at the victim's expense. If he gets caught, he survives for another day at the taxpayer's expense.

Lawyers don't like to defend Slobs. Slobs usually confess and if they don't their alibis or excuses are so unconvincing that the case is hopeless. So they cop a plea. That's why our institutions are full of Slobs and devoid of Slicks.

Once incarcerated a Slob becomes a model prisoner. He adapts easily. He gets comfortable fast. Corrections workers like Slobs, they usually do as they're told. They function well in a structured environment. That's why Slobs oftentimes have good military records but function poorly in a free society where one must make decisions and be responsible for personal freedom.

A Slob is great for any type of rehabilitation. A room full of Slobs will convert to anything—they are an easy sell for alcohol treatment programs or any religious programs, unfortunately their rehabilitation, which is sincere and believed at the time, is short lived. Once they are out of the structured environment they usually revert back to their old irresponsible ways. A Slob is a good candidate for a cult as long as the cult will take care of him.

Our criminal justice system is filled with Slobs. However those who deal with them rarely perceive them as they really are and that is because we confuse them for being Slicks. Slobs front a lot. Fronting is a facade—a play act—a phoney mask to cover up the hollow inadequate person who hides within. Slobs will often put on a disrespectful, belligerent, angry front when confronted with authority. This is often their downfall for it masks and camouflages the low self-worth person who cannot cope with life and its responsibilities. They are perfect "kick-mes". They do everything possible to get society to give them a boot.

Consequently Slobs all across America get hopelessly caught up in the criminal justice system. The courts usually respond to demands of the responsible taxpaying citizens of every community and pack them away. Many judges perceive the Slob as just a lazy belligerent don't-give-a-damn person who simply chooses a life of crime and throws the book at them...packing them away to waste years of their lives at taxpayer's expense. Like tissue to be discarded. The problem is they always return and we are now discovering what we always feared—that maybe we are making them worse rather than better.

It has been said that you can no more cure a criminal in a prison than you can cure a drunk at a local tavern. The place is not conducive to change. It feeds in a negative way the very character defects that cause the criminal his problem in the first place.

WE WANT THEM TO HAVE SELF-WORTH...
So we destroy their self-worth.

WE WANT THEM TO BE RESPONSIBLE...
So we take away all responsibilities.

WE WANT THEM TO BE PART OF OUR COMMUNITY...
So we isolate them from our community.

WE WANT THEM TO BE POSITIVE AND CONSTRUCTIVE...
So we degrade them and make them useless.

WE WANT THEM TO BE TRUST-WORTHY...
So we put them where there is no trust.

WE WANT THEM TO BE NON-VIOLENT...
So we put them where there is violence all around them.

WE WANT THEM TO BE KIND AND LOVING PEOPLE...
So we subject them to hatred and cruelty.

WE WANT THEM TO QUIT BEING THE TOUGH GUY...
So we put them where the tough guy is respected.

WE WANT THEM TO QUIT HANGING AROUND LOSERS...
So we put all the losers in the state under one roof.

WE WANT THEM TO QUIT EXPLOITING US...
So we put them where they exploit each other.

WE WANT THEM TO TAKE CONTROL OF THEIR LIVES, OWN THEIR PROBLEMS AND QUIT BEING A PARASITE...
So we make them totally dependent on us.

It becomes apparent that when we lock up Slobs we are making them worse. This easily explains why the corrections industry has terrible recidivism rates. It's amazing these rates are not higher. If we tried to create a more destructive system for the Slob character disorder we would be hard pressed to do so. If hospitals had as bad a cure rate, we would close them down with a public outcry.

People who do time and go back to prison explain that their prior incarceration does not act as a deterrent. The human mind is great at forgetting the unpleasant, it soon fades into a distant memory, particularly when you view it as bad luck.

Like a new job, the first two or three weeks in prison are the most stressful. Thereafter familiarity and one's comfort zone expands to the new environment, boredom and apathy set in and time goes by...there is nothing to compare it to.

Slicks and Slobs both feel the world is a matter of luck. The haves and the have-nots. The lucky and unlucky. Those who are picked on and those who are not. Neither one of them see themselves as the problem. Slicks fail to see that they are playing a destructive game (let's make a fool out of you) that society will not allow to succeed in the long run. Slobs fail to see that their problem is failure to accept responsibilities, to own their problems and take charge of their lives. Both are irresponsible but in opposite ways. That's the bad news. The good news is they can change. They are not doomed. Many have traveled the road to a responsible life but the change must come from within. No judge, no corrections worker, nobody else can do it for them. They must change themselves. But like travelers who have lost their way, we can give them a roadmap to travel. And with their own free will...they may find the road to responsibility.

AN IRRESPONSIBLE MERRY-GO-ROUND

In every society there are irresponsible criminals who go about being parasites of taxpayers; so the taxpayers hire police to catch them. The police bring the criminals before the judge and jury, who are paid for at taxpayer's expense. The prosecutor, who is paid by taxpayers, argues that the judge should send the criminal off for a long sentence to the state's jails or prisons that are paid for at taxpayer's expense. The public defender, who is paid for by the taxpayers argues that the criminal should get probation to a probation officer who is paid for at taxpayer's expense. The judge who is elected by the taxpayers decides to send the criminal off to prison. After a few years of total dependence on the taxpayers, the criminal is released to live on the streets and to resume being a taxpayer's parasite again. The police arrest him again and the whole merry-go-around starts all over at taxpayer's expense.

No one ever talks about responsibility for wrongdoing. We are simply caught up in a game of deciding where freeloaders are allowed to geographically freeload. We convince ourselves that we are doing justice but we are being taken for a ride at taxpayer's expense. And those who are crime victims get ripped off twice. It's no wonder the average citizen is angry. But, quick solutions such as tougher laws and more punishment make the problem worse rather than better. Negative punishment and responsibility are inconsistent concepts and until we as a society come to this realization, our justice system will continue to fail.

Revenge may be sweet, but it is a costly failure.

Chapter 4

THE DILEMMA OF THE CRIMINAL JUSTICE SYSTEM

It seems that those involved in the corrections system can be divided into two philosophies. The conservative and the liberal. This doesn't relate to Democrats and Republicans or politics in any way. But it appears those who approach the problem with a strong will to dominate, to correct, to control, "to teach them a lesson they will never forget", to make them miserable, to make them conform, fall into the conservative hard-line approach to corrections. On the other side of the coin are those who approach the problem with sympathy, to understand, to rescue, to lend a helping hand, to nurture and comfort, these people seem to fall into the liberal approach to corrections.

Punishing losers simply makes worse losers out of losers. It reinforces their losing characteristics by taking away all responsibilities. Conversely, punishing winners usually makes a better winner out of a winner. When responsible people are punished they respond with responsibility. The Watergate defendants all went on to lead productive lives.

LIBERAL MYTHS

Rescuers on the surface appear to be noble people. They give themselves to helping the less fortunate. They often subscribe to the simplest theory that criminals are the result of unfortunate childhoods and that if you give a loser a chance in life, he will come out all right. Unfortunately in the real world this doesn't work out that way. If you take a winner who is down and out and give him a helping hand he will usually flourish. He knows what responsibility is and will rise to the occasion.

Losers on the other hand have never known what responsibility is and therefore all the helping hands in the world will not bring success. Liberals fall into the same trap as conservatives. They try to *do something to* the loser. The conservatives try to make the loser miserable and the liberals try to make them feel good. Too often liberals believe in programs. "Find the right kind of program for a loser and show them some love and care and they will come out all right."

Both fail to understand the personality of a character disorder.

Unless a person understands responsibility and self-integrity you can add on all the training skills in the world and all that happens is that a dimension is added.

You can take a robber and teach him poetry and the result is a robber whose hold-up notes will rhyme. Teach a stumble-bum burglar how to weld and he'll graduate to safecracking.

On the other hand focusing on a bad characteristic may be illusionary also.

Do-gooders as well as the criminal justice system often get fooled into focusing on the symptom rather than the problem. Losers are adept at shifting the blame onto the symptom such as drugs, alcohol, lousy marriages, lousy parents, the school system, a poor diet...even Twinkies can cause one to kill a mayor in San Francisco.

But at the crux of the matter is irresponsibility. Irresponsible people often drink too much, take drugs, have problems interacting with normal people. But let's not lose focus of the problem.

Many judges are sold the bill of goods that the criminal standing in front of the bench is an alcoholic and that alcohol is the source of his problems. Treatment is the solution. But too often we find that when you take a mean, nasty, dishonest, irresponsible Slob and run him through alcohol treatment you end up with a mean, nasty, dishonest, irresponsible Slob who quit drinking.

When we are irresponsible it is a normal reflex to look around and blame something or someone for our problem. Usually we look around for an "it" to blame it on. It's easier for a motorist who gets a speeding ticket to blame a faulty speedometer or oversized tires than to accept irresponsibility. It is easier to blame booze for your outrageous behavior than to admit that your irresponsible impulses were enhanced and brought out by whiskey. The devil made me do it. When we go down the pathway of life, it is easier to blame the rock for our stumble than to accept responsibility for our clumsy feet.

People all over America get drunk once in a while but very few of them commit crimes simply because they got drunk. But get an irresponsible character disorder drunk and what little self-restraint he has is soon gone.

RESPONSIBILITY VS. ACCOUNTABILITY

A thief breaks into Mr. Jones' home and steals his television. The television is sold to a fence and sometime later the thief is arrested while committing another burglary. The thief is a Slob so he confesses to all his crimes. The judge puts him in jail. The case is closed.

What has happened is the thief was made accountable to society...but not responsible. Mr. Jones is still out his television set and never sleeps the same again. In short the system failed to make the thief undo the wrong he has committed. Accountability but not responsibility.

Courts routinely make criminals accountable... but rarely responsible.

Chapter 5

WORK, FREELOAD, STEAL OR DEAL

For everyone there are only four options of survival. If any person is destitute and is dropped off in any city in any state in America, that person is confronted with the following dilemma: The first option is to find employment, to get a job of some sort in order to receive pay in order to provide a roof over one's head and to feed one's face. If employment is unavailable things get critical and one must resort to handouts or in other words, freeloading. The easiest targets for freeloading are relatives. Relatives always put up with relatives for a short time...usually a short time. Once relatives are used up, the next source is friends, male or female. If the friends are the rescuing type, they will put up with a down and outer for a short period of time. If friends cannot be found who will tolerate a freeloader, then it's off to the Welfare Department for relief. If they turn a person down, it's panhandling off strangers on street corners. Once this fails a person is running out of options for survival within the confines of the law. The next option is to steal. Slicks will con or scheme and Slobs will pull an unsophisticated ripoff, shoplifting, burglary, bad checks, etc. Another option is to deal in drugs or stolen goods. Females can resort to prostitution. In any event stealing and dealing are the last options. There are no other options.

Too often society forgets this simple fact of life. We can take criminals and put them away to teach them a lesson, hoping that the criminal learns his lesson. They walk out of prison (with $100.00 gate money) and are told to sin no more. In their own mind they have repented. They will never, never, never commit a crime again. They will walk the road of righteousness and become a law-abiding citizen.

Then reality sets in.

LAW OF THE STREET

1. GET A JOB
2. FREELOAD
   a) OFF RELATIVES
   b) OFF FRIENDS
   c) GOV'T.- WELFARE
3. DEAL
   a) DRUGS
   b) STOLEN GOODS
   c) PROSTITUTION
4. STEAL
   a) CON-SCHEME
   b) DIRECT RIP-OFF

The ex-convict tries to get a job. After several attempts and rejection he finds that when it comes to filling jobs, employers pass over ex-crooks in favor of anyone else. Why take the chance. Who needs the problem when there are a lot of normal people to choose from. Let someone else hire them. Thus the ex-con must resort to freeloading but to relatives ex-cons are an embarrassment and soon they are on the streets shunned by Welfare (they are able-bodied and perfectly able to work, so they say) and faced with the dangerous two options of stealing or dealing. Mentally they want to stay straight but in terms of harsh reality their options run out. Soon they drift back into crime only to be arrested and the whole process starts all over.

Meanwhile the judge who sentenced them and gave that high-minded morality speech reads about so and so being arrested again and comments to the prosecutor that some people never seem to learn. The trouble is the judge and the ex-convict live in two different worlds with entirely different options. The ex-convict who is usually a Slob is unemployable from the start. Imprisoning an unemployable irresponsible Slob does not change his options. Work, freeload, steal or deal is reality. Promises to go straight soon flicker when hope and self-esteem fade away.

Getting tough on crime is not the solution because being lenient is not the cause of the problem.

THE CATCH 22

Slobs are losers who continue their losing ways, repeating their losing mistakes of thinking and reasoning over and over again. When losers are locked up, punished and degraded, we as society simply reinforce these losing characteristics. In short, we make worse losers out of losers. Rehabilitation in prison is comparable to rehabilitating a drunk by forcing him to the local tavern. Society would be outraged if it was suggested that we should cure alcoholics with more booze, yet taxpayers support more prisons and corrections institutions without question, except as to cost. But there is a Catch 22. We are damned if we do and damned if we don't because if we are nice to Slicks, they'll use us, exploit us and make a fool out of us and laugh at the system. If you are nice to a Slob he will let you take over the problem and by default let you carry him through another day of his irresponsible life. We find ourselves in a no-win dilemma. Thus the constant tug of war back and forth between liberals and conservatives over what to do with criminals continues and continues.

The conservatives want to kick losers till they behave and the liberals want to kiss losers till they behave and neither one works. Both philosophies are failures.

The conseratives are now smugly announcing that the liberals had their chance during the 1960s and 1970s to show the world that crooks could be rehabilitated. The liberals failed. Now it's time to kick rear ends again. They forget that kicking rear ends didn't work either. But they smugly smile, if they are off the street they can't commit crimes...book closed, case over, end of argument. The problem with this simplistic solution is that almost all criminals return to the street sooner or later. If they are made worse, what we have gained momentarily, we dearly pay for down the road. With the Slick the argument has some merit. Slicks are very criminally active and deactivating them does protect society momentarily, however Slicks make up a small amount of our criminals. The problem is that the criminal justice system is inundated with Slobs who subconsciously want to be taken care of and we, by our knee jerk response give them exactly what they want. It's amazing how a hard line conservative will scream with anger at letting an irresponsible Slob be on welfare but will be more than glad to let the Slob be totally supported by the correction system, the ultimate welfare state. When it gets down to the nitty gritty it's all right for a Slob to freeload as long as he doesn't have freedom. But freedom to a Slob is not that wonderful. With freedom comes responsibility and Slobs abhor and shirk responsibility. But the winners who make our laws and perpetuate the criminal justice system are blind to this fact. It's foreign to their thinking.

GOOD INTENTIONS, BAD THEORY

During colonial times in the 18th century, a popular medical method of treating diseases was to bleed the patient. The theory was that diseases were caused by bad blood so it followed that if the doctor (also a part-time barber) drained off some of the bad blood the patient would be able to get better. The bleeding theory was well intended. It made sense to the patient, the doctor and everyone else in the family, unfortunately the cure was in fact killing the patient. It wasn't until Pasteur came along and developed the bacteria theory that medical science gave up this foolish, dangerous bleeding treatment. Medical science soon discovered that we had white corpuscles to fight off the bacteria that invaded our bodies. In short we needed all the blood we had. Unfortunately a lot of people were hurt by this theory. George Washington was bled twice before he died. It probably contributed to his demise. Yet the theory was well intended. The same principle applies to our criminal justice system. Both conservatives and liberals have the same objective but their theories are both wrong and do im-

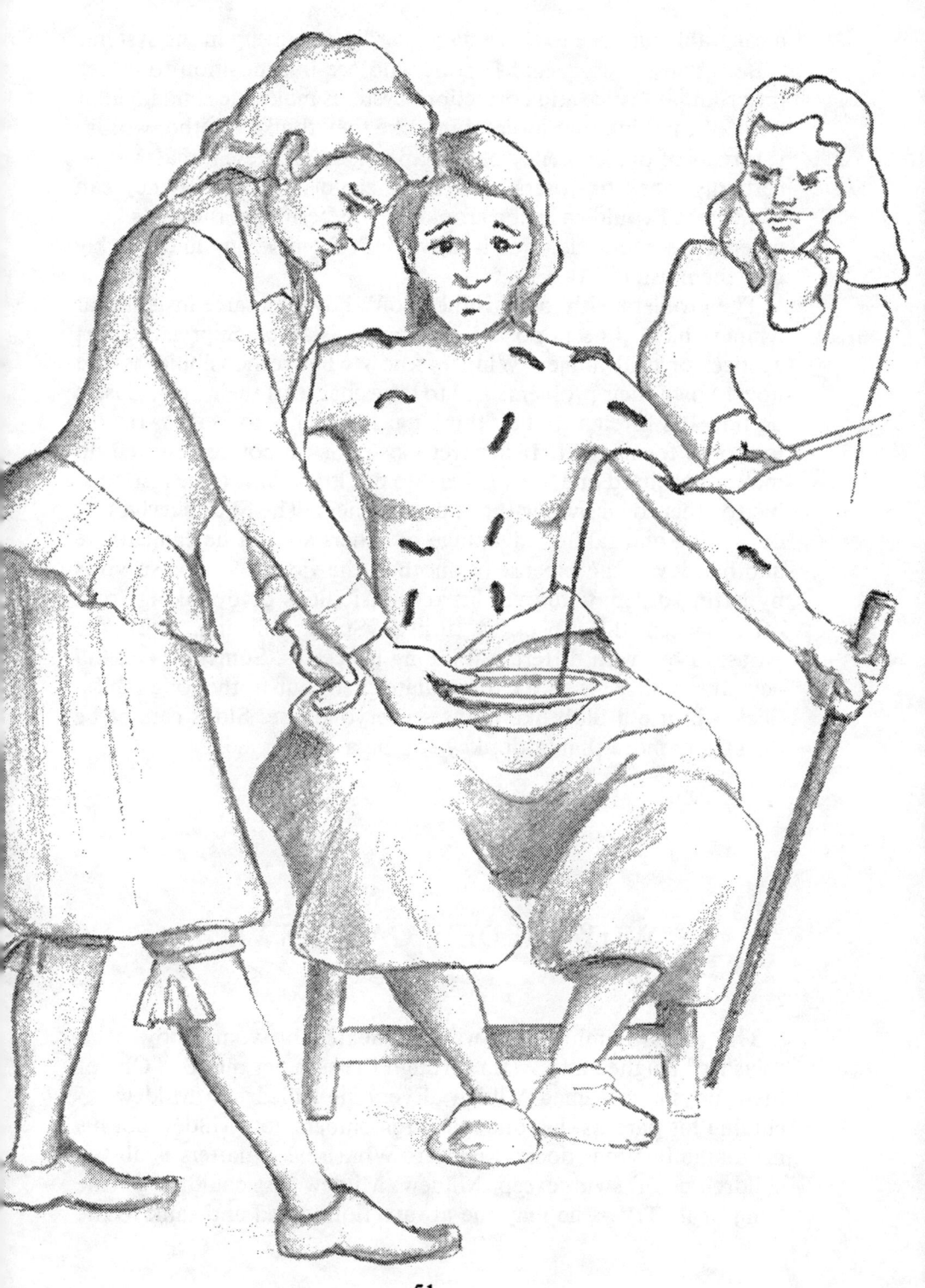

measurable damage to those haphazardly caught up in the system.

Both conservatives and liberals who are in a position to effect the criminal justice and corrections systems make the fundamental error of thinking that losers think like they think. In other words, if threats of punishment would shape them up, these threats would certainly work on losers as well. The old "I made it, they can too," or "I could easily be crooked," or "criminal thoughts have entered my mind also but I know right from wrong and quickly cast them aside."

The problem with losers is they don't have the same insight that winners have. Losers do not become legislators, Supreme Court Justices or trial judges. Winners know what responsibility is and how to own their problems and to take charge of their lives. Losers do not. It's foreign to their thinking. Rehabilitation means restoring to its former self. If it never existed it cannot be restored no matter how hard one tries. Losers do not know how to be responsible for their own lives without using others. The Slick survives by outwitting and taking advantage of others so that he can survive another day at the expense of another, the victim. A Slob survives by letting others take over his responsibilities or by taking from others when their back is turned. Sneak thieving. Both are parasites but with different thinking processes. Sometimes a Slob acts like a Slick, they try to emulate them but in the long haul a Slick will use a Slob like he uses everyone else. Slobs cannot be Slicks any more than a donkey can be a race horse.

WHY MILDEW CAN'T SWIM

The old swimming hole was frequented by young boys who splashed, laughed and swam through the summer months. One of these boys was named Mildew. Everyone called him Mildew including his parents. No one really remembers how Mildew got his nickname but that doesn't matter. What really matters is all the children could swim except Mildew. Mildew just couldn't get the hang of it. Try as he may, he always floundered and sank to the bottom like a rock. The more he tried the more frustrated he became. Soon he just plain quit and sat in despair on the shore. He simply gave up, certain there was something wrong with him that made him different from the rest of the kids. In the world of swimming Mildew was a hopeless loser. The other children couldn't understand why he couldn't swim, because it was so easy for them. Nothing to it...just get in the water and do it. So they would help Mildew and try to teach him but soon they gave up and Mildew forlornly sat on the bank and declared, "Who cares. I don't want to swim anyway." There are "swim haves" and "swim nots" and Mildew was on the short end.

If a hard line conservative would come along he would quickly conclude that there is nothing wrong with Mildew. He just doesn't give a darn. Everyone knows that humans are fully capable of swimming and if one applies himself he will swim...simple as that. "I can swim, so can Mildew." The conservative would then proceed to "correct" Mildew's irresponsible attitude toward swimming by locking him up in a closet for a day. At the end of the day the conservative would let Mildew out and put him in the water. "Are you ready to swim," shouts the conservative. "Yes," cries Mildew, "I have learned my lesson. I will swim." Unfortunately Mildew sinks to the bottom because, as you know, Mildew doesn't know how to swim. So the conservative gets angry and says, "The problem is he isn't trying hard enough. He still doesn't care. He can swim just like me if he tries harder, so we'll double his time in the closet. We will lock him up for two days. One day wasn't enough. He got out too early. He wasn't ready to be rehabilitated yet." So Mildew goes off to the closet for two days. This time he is sure that he will try harder. He concentrates and tells himself, "This time I will swim. I just know it. I can feel it. I shall swim!!" After two days in the closet Mildew is desperate as he is led to the swimming hole. He resolves he will make it this time. Into the pool goes Mildew and with great effort and determination he tries to swim with all the might he can muster, but down he goes. Utter failure, because Mildew doesn't know how to swim and Mildew won't learn how to swim in a closet no matter how long we put him there. So the conservative says, "To hell with him. There are some people who are absolutely useless and you might as well lock them up and throw away the key because they just don't give a damn, that's all." The tissue theory.

Along comes a rescuing liberal. He says, "It's obvious that you can't teach Mildew how to swim by locking him up in a closet. Poor Mildew, he's never had a chance in life. How can you expect someone who grew up on a desert and never had an opportunity to be around water to be able to swim. What we've got to do is give him a chance, an opportunity in life to swim like us who are more fortunate. I know how to swim so I'll give him a chance to be like me." So the liberal jumps into the water and swims across the pool and says, "See, there is nothing to it." The liberal then puts his arm around Mildew and pulls Mildew across the pool and puts Mildew's hands on the other side. "See, nothing to it, you made it all the way across."

Mildew shakes his head and says, "Not really, it looks like I swam across the pool but really you swam for me. I just came along for the ride." "Aw, close enough," says the liberal, "Come on, we're going to take you down to the employment office and get you a CETA job as a lifeguard."

PEOPLE CHANGE FROM WITHIN AND RESIST CHANGE FROM WITHOUT

THE WAY OUT OF THE DILEMMA

We don't change people, people change themselves. Change must come from within. But change comes from within only when people want to change. If people are unhappy enough and dissatisfied with their lives to the point they want to change, then change will occur. If people are comfortable and willing to accept their status quo, then they will remain dormant, doomed to repeat their errors over and over.

If low self-worth is their problem then they must change their self-image. If irresponsibility is their problem then they must acquire for themselves the concept of responsibility. If they feel alienated from the community and the mainstream of society then they must find their way into the community and join society instead of ripping it off like a parasite.

If they have committed destructive acts then they must find ways to do constructive acts—positive acts to offset their negative acts.

If they don't want to own their problem and choose to remain passive and dormant, we must learn how to make them uncomfortable enough so they will want to change and take charge of their lives and be responsible to themselves and others.

The most important step is that losers must come to the realization that they are their own problem, that their viewpoint of life is twisted and irresponsible. They must be able to step back and see themselves for what they are. Our present justice system fails to provide avenues or the means to encourage change. In fact, it unwittingly does exactly the opposite. It cultivates irresponsibility.

WHERE'S THE SHEEP?

The illustration on the next page depicts a sheep. Some will quickly see it, others will not, no matter how hard they try.

Sometimes our minds quickly make sense out of chaos, other times we give up in frustration. But, until we "get the picture," we remain in a state of stress and anxiety. We either try harder to understand, get help to point the way or we give up in despair and tell ourselves: Who gives a damn, anyway. To those of us who easily see the picture, we become impatient with those who don't see the picture. Losers don't get the picture and remain dormant. They cannot change because they don't know how. They don't know they have a problem. We assume they see the picture when they do not have the slightest concept of what's wrong. What is clear to us is obscure to them.

Slicks do not see themselves as being capricious. In fact, they see themselves as being superior, smarter and quicker than the rest of the world. What they are oblivious to is that they survive by taking away the fruits and labor of others by unfair and dishonest means.

But to them that's normal. Slicks see the world as a rat race where everyone rips off each other. Dog eat dog. To him there is no difference between himself and the average businessman. The businessman is simply more subtle, the Slick is more bold and exciting. The businessman rips people off and gets away with it. The criminal Slick is just unlucky enough to get caught once in a while, so reasons the Slick. That's why prison newspapers always carry newsclippings of police who are arrested for crimes, a judge who is bribed or a corporation that gets busted for ripping off the public. It proves to Slicks that the rest of the world is as rotten as they are, they just are unfortunate enough to get caught. Next time they're going to be a lot smarter. The error in this reasoning is clear. Most people are honest and responsible but the Slick chooses to see only what he wants to see. To a Slick honest and responsible people are fools and suckers who are doomed to boring lives. But a Slick never wants to realize that if he's so damn smart why is he where he is—a locked-up loser.

Slobs on the other hand have never learned to be self-sufficient, to stand on their own two feet, and therefore they lean on others. They survive from day to day absorbing the labors of others. A Slob sees himself as unfortunate and inadequate. There are superior people and inferior people and he happens to be on the losing end, life is not going to get better but will continue to be more of the same. It's a world of 'have' and 'have nots' and if a 'have not' rips off a 'have' now and then it only evens out the unfairness of it all.

Slobs must learn to take charge of their lives, stand on their own feet and own their problems. Slicks have got to learn that they can become responsible, useful citizens in the legitimate business world without taking dishonest shortcuts.

Chapter 6

RESTITUTION

Most judges will tell you they see many more Slobs in court than Slicks. Probably a ten to one ratio is not an exaggeration. Since Slobs are abundant and clog up the criminal justice system the most, they will be considered first. The Slob's problem in a nutshell is as follows.

If irresponsibility is a Slob's problem then judges should make them accountable. Locking up a Slob makes them irresponsible and society becomes totally accountable for every aspect of their lives. We totally take over their obligations and the victim of a Slob's crime loses his property and shares the cost of supporting him while incarcerated. We make freeloaders out of a freeloader. It has not always been that way. Our ancestors knew what responsibility was, either they became productive and self-sufficient or they perished. Simple as that, unless they could find a benefactor.

Character Defect	Counter Measures
1. Irresponsible	Restitution
2. Alienated	Community Service
3. Avoids Problem	Owns Problem
4. Low Self-Image	Self-Image Change
5. Destructive	Constructive

A common myth in America is that jails and prisons always existed in one form or another. It's simply not true. The first prison used for rehabilitation purposes was built on Walnut Street in Philadelphia less than 200 years ago (1790). Unfortunately, colonial Slobs and Slicks didn't rehabilitate any better then than they do now. Probation came about in 1840 as an alternative to the horrible prisons. What we have lost track of or what faded out of the criminal justice system was the ancient concept of restitution. The early settlers of the West came about restitution naturally. There simply were no local jails, judges or probation officers around, so social pressures created restitution spontaneously. Wrongdoers either made it right with the victim or they were socially or physically banished from the community. Simple rural, backwoods justice.

The concept of restitution is an old concept going back to the time of Moses and before. There are records of restitution justice in ancient Egypt. The Law of Moses required that the victim not only be compensated for his loss but that the victim be overpaid three, four or five times the loss. The modern legal concept of treble damages comes from the ancient concept of restitution.

DINING AND DASHING

After the taverns closed, a group of college students thought it was funny to go into a restaurant and charge a big meal and then sneak out the back door without paying the tab. They called it "dining and dashing." The students thought it great fun and laughed all the way back to their dormitories. The restaurant owners saw little humor in the thieving. One night the police were waiting at the back door and four young men were escorted to jail to await their appearance before the local judge. The next morning they soberly appeared in court and pled guilty to theft.

"Gentlemen," said the judge, "Theft has always been against the rules of civilized society. You found yourselves in jail this morning and if you want to get out of jail you are going to have to be responsible. This court will apply the ancient Law of Moses, set down more than four thousand years ago. Moses said if you stole a sheep you must give back four sheep...you shall make restitution." The judge asked the young men, "How much was the tab at the restaurant that you skipped out on?" A member of the group answered, "Twenty dollars." The judge responded, "Then the sentence of this court is that you shall go to the restaurant owner and pay him four times the amount you have taken. Pay

EXODUS 1

22 And Joseph dwelt in Egypt, he, and his father's house: and Joseph lived an hundred and ten years.

23 And Joseph saw E′-phra-im's children of the third *generation:* the children also of Ma′-chir the son of Ma-nas′-seh were brought up upon Joseph's knees.

24 And Joseph said unto his brethren, I die: and God will surely visit you, and bring you out of this land unto the land which he sware to Abraham, to Isaac, and to Jacob.

25 And Joseph took an oath of the children of Israel, saying, God will surely visit you, and ye shall carry up my bones from hence.

26 So Joseph died, *being* an hundred and ten years old: and they embalmed him, and he was put in a coffin in Egypt.

The Second Book of Moses, called

Exodus

CHAPTER 1

NOW these *are* the names of the children of Israel, which came into Egypt; every man and his household came with Jacob.

2 Reuben, Simeon, Levi, and Judah,

3 Is′-sa-char, Zeb′-u-lun, and Benjamin,

4 Dan, and Naph′-ta-li, Gad, and Asher.

5 And all the souls that came out of the loins of Jacob were seventy souls: for Joseph

6 A breth

7 fru and mig ther

8 over

9 hold Isra we:

10 them; le

to pass, that, when any war, they join also enemies, and fight against us, and so get them up out of the land.

11 Therefore they did set over them taskmasters to afflict them with their burdens. And they built for Pharaoh treasure cities, Pi′-thom and Ra-am′-ses.

12 But the more they afflicted them, the more they multiplied and grew. And they were grieved because of the children of Israel.

13 And the Egyptians made the children of Israel to serve with rigour:

14 And they made their lives bitter with hard bondage, in morter, and in brick, and in all manner of service in the field: all their service, wherein they made them serve, *was* with rigour.

15 And the king of Egypt spake to the Hebrew midwives, of which the name of the one *was* Shiph′-rah, and the name of the other Pu′-ah:

16 And he said, When ye do the of a midwife to the Hebrew stools; but live. od, hil-

for em, ve

to en for ere em.

erefore well with the midwives: and the people multiplied, and waxed very mighty.

21 And it came to pass, because the midwives feared God, that he made them houses.

22 And Pharaoh charged all his people, saying, Every son that is born ye shall cast into the river, and every daughter ye shall save alive.[1]

> "If a man steals an ox or a sheep, and kills it or sells it, he shall pay five oxen for the ox, or four sheep for a sheep. He shall make restitution. . . ."
>
> — Exodus 22:1, 2

him $80.00. You must then get a receipt from him and bring it back to this court. If you do so, no further fine or jail sentence will be ordered." The young men agreed and as they were leaving, the judge stopped them and asked, "Did you receive good service from the waiter or waitress?" "Yes, she was a good waitress," replied the young men. "Then find her and pay her 20% of $80.00 and file a receipt with the court," ordered the judge.

Moses strikes again.

Thereafter the judge was invited to attend a restaurant owners association meeting to discuss this novel approach. The judge asked how many "diners and dashers" were caught during a normal college year.

"We figure about one out of four gets caught. The other three get away."

"That makes sense," replied the judge. "That's why old Moses made it four to one."

INDIAN JUSTICE

The North American Indians had a unique criminal justice system that served them well. It was pure restitution justice. The victim of a crime was compensated by the wrongdoer. Not only was a thief required to pay back for what had been taken, but over-compensation was expected.

If a young Indian juvenile delinquent was stealing, the thief was brought before the chief and the tribal council to make it right. Obviously the wrongdoer wasn't locked in a wigwam for 30 days. That would make no sense to the Indians. Why render a person useless when everyone was necessary for survival. Nor would they place him on probation to a medicine man to report once a moon. That would be equally ridiculous. In fact, most Indian tribes would never have thought of such useless ways of dealing with a wrongdoer. The white man's justice of degrading a person or making them lose face would not be natural to the Indian way of respecting human dignity. The criminal would be expected to

"make it right" with the victim and once this was accomplished the matter was closed and life went on as it should. The penalty for refusing to "make it right" would be social ostracism and ultimately banishment. However, once a banished person chose to be responsible, the banishment would be lifted and the wrongdoer would be allowed back into the community. The Sioux Indians routinely used community service as a method of making it right with the rest of the tribe for transgressions that jeopardized the tribe's well-being.

The American justice system would do well to absorb the simplistic, pure justice system of the Native American Indian. Instead, the Native Americans have been tragically absorbed into our present system and their superior system has all but disappeared.

RESTITUTION AND VIOLENT CRIME

Traditionally restitution has never applied to violent offenders. Murder, rape and physical brutality must be met with incarceration, not because it cures violence but simply because incareration will protect society. However, violent crime is less than 5% of all crime.

THE BASIC PRINCIPLE OF RESTITUTION

Restitution means making it right, being accountable to those who have been harmed. Slobs don't understand responsibility so it is important that they be subjected to a dose of accountability.

Victims have long been neglected in our criminal justice system.

It is time we bring back the ancient concept of restitution to our modern society and include in almost all sentences provisions for repayment for the harm done by the wrongful acts of criminals.

The victim should not only be repaid but overpaid. The difference or excess is part of the punishment and it brings home the message of responsibility. The punishment, however, is constructive and productive, not a drain on society like incarceration.

Criminals cost society money...tax money. The criminal justice system is a drain on society. The law enforcement agencies, the court system, the insurance industry, all are supported by tax dollars or premiums. It only makes sense that those who make the system necessary should pay back society in a general sense. That's why community service is such a natural consequence. The offender can contribute to society rather than ripping it off. Putting something back...making a right for a wrong...a positive for a negative.

Slobs don't feel they are part of society. Community service allows them to join society in a responsible productive way. Remember, Slobs don't know what it is to be responsible so a little responsible labor that helps society is the first step toward getting a glimpse of the sheep. Slobs want to be rescued but nobody can perform community service for them so they are caught up being accountable, like it or not.

The third component of restitution justice is self-responsibility, doing something productive and constructive for oneself. Slobs are dormant, stagnant people and our present criminal justice system seems hellbent on keeping the status quo by making dependents out of parasites. Slobs are passive people caught up in their own losing mentality. It is absolutely necessary that they get going in life. People change themselves by self-motivation, so Slobs must be made uncomfortable enough to want to change. Most restitution sentences in American courts completely forget this component.

BASIC PRINCIPLE OF RESTITUTION

IF *YOU* HAVE WRONGED SOMEONE IT IS

YOUR RESPONSIBILITY TO MAKE IT RIGHT WITH THAT PERSON AND TO *YOUR* COMMUNITY AS A WHOLE BY POSITIVE, CONSTRUCTIVE ACTS AND IT IS *YOUR* RESPONSIBILITY TO IMPROVE *YOURSELF* WITH PERSONAL ACHIEVEMENTS AND GOALS.

PUT UP OR BE LOCKED UP

All restitution sentences should be an alternative to punishment or jail. In other words, if an offender wants to work himself around and out of a jail sentence, he must become answerable to the victim, the community and himself. If he or she fails to be responsible, then they have bought the punishment of incarceration. The offender must clearly understand that he can save himself from the slammer only if he performs within the time limits that are negotiated with the court. Put up or be locked up. However, once the offender has lived up to his end of the bargain and has completed the restitution sentence, he should be immediately discharged from the system to resume, hopefully, a normal life. No probation to the medicine man or second-rate citizen status. The offender has earned his right to be treated as a normal citizen.

RESTITUTION TO VICTIM
1. Pay the Damages
2. Repair the Damages
3. Alternate Work for Victim

RESTITUTION TO COMMUNITY
1. Charitable Agencies
2. City, County Government
3. Educational Institutions
4. Parks, Rivers, Lakes and Ecology
5. Handicapped and Elderly
6. Church

RESTITUTION TO OFFENDER
1. Alcohol and Drug Counseling
2. Vocational, College, High School
3. Mental Health Center
4. Marriage Counseling
5. Vocational Rehabilitation
6. Employment Counseling
7. Community Activities
8. Church Activities

RESTITUTION TO THE VICTIM

Most crimes have victims. Some do not. If there is a victim, the offender should pay the direct loss, usually in the form of cash. The victim should be paid in full and in some cases double, triple or quadruple the loss sustained. Sometimes this is unreasonable or unattainable; but in any event, the victim should be made whole as soon as possible. If the victim is agreeable and the loss is in the form of property damage, such as vandalism, the offender should repair the damages. If the victim prefers a professional repair job, then the offender should pay the repair bill. If the offender cannot raise the money, then the possibility of alternative work of a different nature but of equal value can be performed.

An example: A store owner's window was vandalized. The store owner preferred to have a glass repairman fix it but agreed that the offender could clean and paint his basement to offset the cost.

RESTITUTION TO THE COMMUNITY

In any town, city or rural area, many deeds can be performed that improve the community. Allowing losers to perform community service accomplishes two objectives. It puts something positive, constructive and humanitarian back into society and at the same time it allows a loser to join society. Losers don't feel part of society, so let's let them join instead of banishing them to freeload at taxpayers' expense.

Any organization that qualifies as a non-profit association can be utilized as a source for community service.

CHARITIES

Across America losers can donate their time to charitable organizations. The telephone directory yellow pages are full of charities; the Chamber of Commerce has a list of United Fund agencies and many more. Donating blood to the Red Cross, setting up bloodmobile drives, the American Cancer Society, Crippled Childrens' Fund, the list can go on and on.

THE GOVERNMENT

Since all government subdivisions, be they Federal, State, County, City, Village or Township, all are tax supported, any work donated to local government helps ease the burden of the taxpayers. Painting government buildings, repairing damage done by vandals; the streets and highways all need shaping up, and law breakers are in unlimited supply to do the job. Some citizens say they are taking jobs away from law-abiding citizens. This is a narrow view, as any local government always has work it can't get to, low priority work that needs to be done but funds are not available. These make perfect job sites for community service restitution.

THE EDUCATION INSTITUTIONS

Public, private schools, and colleges are always short of funds. There is an abundance of maintenance work that can be found for young offenders.

THE RIVERS, LAKES, PARKS AND ECOLOGY

Our environment is constantly being threatened by pollution. Picking up litter on the banks of rivers and lakes, maintaining parks and cleaning up roadsides are all obvious work sites. Sportsmen's clubs always have projects to help wildlife. Planting trees and working with the Forestry Service, the Department of Natural Resources or other environmental agencies are all potential places for losers to help join society.

THE HANDICAPPED AND ELDERLY

Every community has disadvantaged people who can use help. Elderly homes always have projects requiring contributions of time and effort. Those who are either temporarily or permanently handicapped, need to be helped to get around and they need to have errands run for them. Direct contact with less fortunate people can only be constructive to people with low self-esteem.

THE CHURCHES

Churches survive on meager contributions. Offenders can always find work that needs to be done in the church facilities or church projects. Churches should be the first to reach out to transgressors. The clergy will usually respond but the criminal justice system never asks them. The possibilities are endless.

SELF RESTITUTION

Character disorders, be they Slicks or Slobs, have got to get out of their losing ways. But no one is going to do it for them, they must do it for themselves. Every meaningful restitution sentence should include self-help as an alternative to incarceration. Self-help can be alcohol and drug counseling, joining Alcoholics Anonymous, in-patient treatment or any program aimed at confronting the problem.

Mental health counseling, psychological evaluations, marriage counseling, employment counseling, vocational rehabilitation, taking a course at a vocational school, college or completing high school are all self-help options. Perhaps joining the human race is all that is needed. This can be accomplished by getting involved with community or church activities.

The potential activities available are too numerous to mention, but any creative corrections worker could post on the wall of his or her office hundreds of alternatives for any loser to choose from...like a smorgasbord buffet dinner.

GETTING LOSERS MOTIVATED

First of all, losers have to be made uncomfortable enough to want to motivate themselves to be responsible. They must understand that it's jail or responsibility, not go home and be a nice guy probation, but old-fashioned responsibility time is upon them. If they choose jail (some will), then they will remain a useless stagnant Slob. If they want to earn themselves out of the mess they are in, then the opportunity must be given to do so.

GETTING SLOBS OFF DEAD CENTER

An old judge once said, "You will never go wrong if you treat people the same way as you would want them to treat you if you were in their shoes."

If we treat people as children, they will respond as children. If we treat people as responsible adults, they usually respond as responsible adults.

Confront and be critical of a person's acts, but do not attack the person. We all may admit we made a fool of ourselves on occasion, but we all flash in anger at being made a fool of.

Our courts traditionally put people down and make them feel inferior. We purposely create a parent-child relationship. The judge wears a black robe. The bench is elevated and rituals are observed with salutations of "Your Honor". The judge becomes the all-powerful father figure and the offender becomes the wayward child. The corrections workers all become parents who "supervise", "order", "set down rules", "monitor" and "bust" the violator when they don't follow the dictates of the court.

This system was obviously created by winners and responsible people who, with good intentions, felt that when people behave as children they must be disciplined into shape and taught some respect for what is right in this world. And for normally responsible winners it works. They know what responsibility is and a little reminder will get them back on track. The problem is it utterly fails on losers because they never were responsible, they never have stood on their own feet. Losers survive by irresponsibility, using other people to survive for another day. The courts start out on the wrong foot with losers and we lose the game before we start.

No one likes to be put down, belittled, degraded or to be made to appear foolish. We become angry at being made to look inferior (see illustration). Those of us who know we are normal can survive because we know we are not inferior and that we can weather the storm. We will get back our respectability by responding in a responsible manner. Losers don't have this option. They have never felt respected except by a negative peer group, a group having low status in our society. A shallow respect. It is fundamental that when someone "comes on" with a parental superior attitude, the other person who is confronted will automatically feel or experience the feeling we had when we were children.

An authoritarian who orders us around, sets down the rules, and "knows what's best for us" will bring out feelings of anger, defiance, helplessness or inadequacy in us and we will respond accordingly with capitulation or defiance.

THROUGH THE EYES OF A LOSER

A pompous, self-satisfied, authoritarian judge is asked to speak to a civic organization about juvenile delinquency. The audience is looking for his guidance. About halfway through the judge's presentation, a man walks in late and sits down in the back of the room. The judge stops and stares at the latecomer, puts his hand on his hips, fixes his eyes on the man, points his finger and says in a loud voice: "You're late! I started this lecture at eight o'clock and here it is nine o'clock already and in you walk. If anyone in this building needs to know what is being presented here, it is you!"

If the latecomer is a Slob, he will hang his head and apologize for being late, using the words "yes, sir" as much as possible. He will make excuses, attempting to find something to blame, a bad clock, misinformation, went to the wrong building, his mother didn't remind him, etc. In his mind he tells himself, "Here I go again. I always goof up. Nothing ever comes out right for me, bad luck, etc." He hopes someone will come to his rescue and smooth it out for him. The Slob feels inadequate so he looks at the floor and hopes it will all pass over, but everything that happens confirms the fact that he is inferior, he is a loser—what's the use, life always turns out this way.

On the other hand, suppose the latecomer is a Slick. He will glare back at the judge and say to himself, "Don't put me down, you S.O.B." and stand up and shake his fist at the speaker and shout, "Aw, go to hell, you pompous old fool. You're lucky I showed up at all. You don't know what the hell you're talking about anyway. Who needs your crap," and walks out and slams the door. In his mind there is anger and he says to himself, "That old scum bucket tried to make a fool out of me. I'll show him. I'll get him, I'll slash his tires and teach that stupid scumbag not to mess with me." Slicks don't take constructive criticism well, they just get even.

But let's suppose the latecomer is the type of person who has it all together and is not caught up in any games and responds: "I have certain priorities in my life. One of my priorities was to be here and listen to your presentation. Unfortunately, I have other important things in my life that take up my time also. Apparently people who show up late to your lectures irritate you and make you angry. That's your probblem and not mine. I'm not going to buy into your problem. I wish you would stop taking up everyone's time with your problems and continue your presentation. I'm interested in what you have to say, otherwise I wouldn't be here...late, but, nevertheless, I'm here."

The manner in which we treat people greatly influences their responses. If the person we are dealing with comes into the transaction with a preconceived notion, the result will be totally affected by the preconceived notion.

When a winner is confronted by an authoritarian or a parental figure, such as a judge or police officer, for a mistake or wrongdoing, the mental reactions are normal and non-threatening. The winner thinks to himself: "Yeah, I made a mistake. I'll correct it...I'm glad the judge pointed that out to me...I've got to be more responsible...This isn't the way I normally behave...I've straightened out my life before, I'll do it again...I'm not a loser...I'll show them that I'm in charge of my life...What I did was stupid, I should have known better...I've hurt innocent people and that's not right...I shouldn't take stupid chances...This is not like me, they are getting the wrong impression of me...I'm embarrassed...I'll make it right."

When a Slick is confronted by an authority figure for a wrongdoing, there is a different reaction: "Aw, get off my back...who the hell do you think you are...You're just as bad as me only you're getting by with your stuff...Don't mess with me...You lean on me too much and you'll wish you hadn't...I'm smarter than you are, you just lucked out or someone gave you a silver spoon...So I hurt someone, so what, the sucker had it coming...I got to figure a way out of this mess...I'll go along with your game if it will get me out of this mess...idiots...who you fooling. You're not smart enough to get the best of me...Don't mess with my Constitutional rights...I'll get my lawyer to say...I've gotten out of messes like this before, I'll do it again...I'll tell them what they want to hear."

Slobs, on the other hand, have a different mental response: "Well, here I go again...I always screw up...It's the story of my life...Lousy luck...If I only hadn't listened to those guys I wouldn't be in this mess...It's their fault, not mine...Why don't the cops leave me alone...At the time it was a good idea; I guess I never think of the consequences until it comes down on me...Life is a bummer...You're right; I am a loser...I'll shape up this time...If only...Nobody ever does anything for me; everyone else gets everything given to them...I suppose I'll get the maximum...I don't blame them for being angry at me...If someone would have helped me this wouldn't have happened...What do people expect when...If I cooperate with them it will go easier...If they hadn't got me so drunk it wouldn't have happened...Every time I think I'm going to lose her I go bonkers...It's just not fair...The cops are picking on me...Why are they always on my rear end...Those other guys are no better than me, yet they always get away with it...Sometimes life is not worth living...I suppose they'll lock me up again; but what the hell, I've been through that before, it's not so bad...Now see what you made me go and do."

When we come on as an authoritarian to a Slob we simply make him feel like he is a loser. We bring out the worst in him.

When we come on as an authoritarian to a Slick, we are simply setting up a game, a challenge to see if he can get the best of us, make a fool out of us and prove he's smarter than we are. That's his whole life's pattern and this pattern goes on and on.

The answer lies in confronting losers with being responsible and taking charge of their lives, which means, quit being a parasite on others and stand on your own two feet, own your problems and to realize that only you can change yourself. We must say to them, "If you are responsible, we will treat you with fairness and with decency that you deserve as an equal, responsible person. If you don't take charge of your life then we will take over your life and you won't like the results."

"We can't change you but we can make you miserable, dormant and hopeless. It's up to you, the ball is in your court."

Putting this concept to work is not easy. The corrections people in control must rewire their brains and learn some new common sense concepts.

First, criminal court judges have got to stop thinking like judges. They must constantly be aware that the person standing in front of them, if that person is a chronic loser, doesn't use the same thinking process that the judge does. The judge and his corrections officers must first determine whether they have a normally responsible person who made a mistake or are they looking at a Slick or a Slob.

The normally responsible person who made a mistake will readily change himself and get back on the constructive, responsible, winning side of life. Restitution sentences are perfect for him. Short jail sentences with the opportunity to prove he is accountable are all that is necessary. Judges can easily relate to this type of offender. The typical white-collar criminal falls into this category. Most judges feel sorry for white-collar criminals because they usually lose their jobs and the wife and kids suffer. White-collar criminals usually receive light sentences involving probation.

Where criminal court judges completely miss the boat is when they deal with the Slick or Slob. The judge sits on the bench and thinks he has great insight into his fellow man (where this came from is a mystery because most judges lack psychological training). By osmosis, the judge has acquired this remarkable ability. He then proceeds to give a sentence that he is sure would work on himself if he were in similar circumstances. He leaves the bench, satisfied that he has done all that can be done, when, in fact, he probably did more harm than good.

The average legislator falls into the same trap. Legislators are winners and when they arrive at the state capitol, they are going to make some changes in a criminal justice system that obviously needs changing. Those blind judges just don't know what they are doing, which may be true, but at least the judge knows from daily experience that the legislator's half-baked theories won't work. What does work is a mystery to the judge because he's been down the path of being lenient and getting burned and being tough and not succeeding either. Both the average legislator and judge make the same mistake—they don't understand how a loser thinks and they make the same mistake over and over.

PUTTING THE PROBLEM ONTO THE PERSON WHO HAS THE PROBLEM

If we are going to have any success with a loser (Slick or Slob), we must make them own their problem. Across America every day, losers are paraded in front of judges who stare down at them and commence to take over their lives.

"You have wronged us, therefore, here is what I am going to do to you!"

"You have wronged us, therefore, here is what I am going to do to you," says the man in the black robe.

The judge then, without question as to its validity, proceeds to pronounce sentence. After all, isn't that what judges have been doing for centuries. Isn't that what a judge is for. The judge then sends the offender off to jail. (Teach them a lesson they will never forget, even though it didn't work the last time for the same mistake. After they are released, they will be on probation for a number of years—that didn't work last time either).

What happens is the loser is under the complete control of the system. The judge owns the problem and is prescribing the cure. The offender is not in charge of his life, doesn't own his problems and is given no opportunity to become responsible for his wrongdoing. Instead, society owns his problems and has completely taken over his life and all the responsibilities that go with it, exactly the problem a Slob suffers from the most: Lack of responsibility and a failure to own his own problems.

What we must do is reverse this everyday philosophy of the criminal courts and put the ball in the loser's court. Judges must get across the following concept:

> "The question is not what are we going to do to you; but rather, what are you going to do to make it right?"

IT'S YOUR PROBLEM

A young man named Jones was having an argument with his girlfriend in front of a movie theatre. The argument got more heated, and suddenly the man pushed the young lady away, swore at her and proceeded to walk away in anger. As he proceeded down the sidewalk, he reached out and snapped off the radio antennas of parked cars. After he had succeeded in breaking off eight antennas, a witness shouted at him and the vandal fled before the police could be summoned. The police soon identified who the perpetrator was from information given by the girlfriend. The vandal was found in a bar a few blocks away, arrested and taken into custody. The next day he appeared in court and pled guilty to criminal damage to property.

The Judge: Why did you destroy the property of people who have done you no harm?

Jones: I do dumb things when I'm angry. I guess I just didn't give a darn at the time. Now I'm sorry it happened.

The Judge: You have created a problem, what are you going to do about the problem?

Jones: I'll pay for the damages.

The Judge: That's fine. Do you have any money?

Jones: I've saved up some money for our wedding but I guess that's not coming off. I also can earn some money.

The Judge: Officer do you have some police reports that identify the victims of this crime?

Police Officer: We have police reports but the problem is the cars that were damaged were all parked in front of the theatre and after the movie was over, everyone got into their cars and left. Apparently no one checked their radio antennas before they left. They would have no reason to do so.

The Judge: Mr. Jones, you have a problem.

Jones: I'll find them and make it right with them. I'll apologize also.

The Judge: That's the problem, Mr. Jones, it may not be easy to find these victims without considerable effort.

Jones: I know, but I'll try hard.

The Judge: That's right, I want you to devote full time attention to this problem. It's your problem and it should consume 100% of your time and energy.

Jones: Oh, yes, it will, I will assure you.

The Judge: That's why I'm going to lock you up in jail for 45 days, starting right now, and as soon as you find these eight people you have wronged and have paid them in full, I'll release you immediately. If you do it today, you'll be set free today. If it takes you a week, you'll be let out in a week. Simple as that. It's your problem. It's up to you to perform or sit the entire 45 days.

Jones: But, Judge, how can I find these people if I'm locked up in jail?

The Judge: I don't know. You created the problem, you solve it. I don't go about vandalizing people's radio antennas, so I can't give you much advice. I have no experience with problems like you have.

The incredulous defendant was led off to jail. The next day an ad appeared in the local newspaper that read:

> <u>Notice to the Public.</u> I need your help.
> If you have sustained damages to your car's radio antenna recently, please call the county jail and ask for John Jones. I will pay for your damages. Please respond. I desperately need to hear from you. Call day or night, Tel. 452-2383

Forty-four people responded to the ad. Mr. Jones did not know what to do. He couldn't pay them all. There were only eight victims. He needed to talk to the judge, so the jailer returned him to court.

The Judge: Do you have a problem, Mr. Jones?

Jones: Yes, I do, they're trying to rip me off. All forty-four of them want to be paid.

The Judge: You've got a problem.

Jones: I know, which ones do I pay?

The Judge: I don't know, it's not my problem. I've never been in a situation like you are in.

At this time a Court Services officer spoke up and said: I'll help him sort out the claims.

The Judge: No, you won't. It's not your problem. He created the problem, not you. Go rescue someone who has some genuine hard luck, not those who have created their own problems by their own irresponsibility.

So, the defendant Jones was, once again, led off to jail in utter frustration. He then concluded that his newspaper ad was too broad in its meaning. He had not specifically tied down the date in question. People were making claims for antennas that were lost months ago. After processing each claim and getting the facts down with phone calls, he found that four of the claims were valid and were the result of his malicious acts. They were paid in full. In the meantime, four days had passed and Jones was getting desperate. He wanted to talk and plead with the judge again. Back to court he was taken.

The Judge: You have a problem, Mr. Jones?

Jones: Yes, Your Honor, I have located four of the eight people I owe damages to. I can't find anymore, so I suggest that I deposit $400.00 with the court and if anyone turns up, you can pay them with this money.

The Judge: Then we will own your problem. It's not our problem; it's your problem.

Jones: But what should I do; I can't find them.

The Judge: Try harder, put more energy into your problem.

Once again, Jones was led away to the jail. After many hours of contemplating, suddenly a light bulb went off in his head. Claims adjusters! He raced to the telephone and with the help of the yellow pages he began to call anyone who had anything to do with automobile insurance. Sure enough, after two days he located three more of his victims. Just one person to find. That person out there somewhere had the key to his cell. Jones was getting frantic. He was at his wits end. He had to talk to the judge again and plead once more.

The Judge: You have a problem, Mr. Jones?

Jones: I've found 7 of the 8 people with cars I damaged. It's taken me a week, but I paid them all back. I think I've done as well as can be expected under the circumstances. Can't I be released now?

The Judge: Somewhere out there among 50,000 people is a person who has a problem replacing an antenna that you broke off. You created his or her problem. It's only right that you find that person. You created the problem. Solve the problem.

So back to jail went Jones. After another day of anxiety and frustration, it suddenly occurred to Jones that he was in a border town and that just across the river was another state. Maybe the car came from out-of-state. He began calling claims adjusters and, sure enough, he came up with another person who had lost an antenna on the night of his arrest. He promptly paid the lady. The sheriff, after consulting with the judge, let Jones free. It had taken him a week to find all eight victims, but he found them. On the way out the door, he turned to the jailer and said, "I'm getting out of this darn county. That judge is crazy!"

What the judge did was foreign to the justice system. He made a

"I have wronged someone and this is what I offer to make it right."

criminal be responsible for his crime. He put the problem onto the person who created the problem. Therein lies part of the solution of dealing with Slicks and Slobs. Jones learned responsibility the hard way.

Getting irresponsible people to be responsible isn't easy, particularly when the world is full of rescuers. Rescuing unfortunate people is admirable as long as the unfortunate cannot rescue themselves. But Slobs do not fall into this category. Slobs are perfectly able to help themselves, they simply have never learned how to be responsible and have learned to get by, day to day, letting someone else carry their load. Slobs need enablers, someone to lean on or take over their problems, take over their obligations. As long as they have an enabler, they will generally remain crime free; but if they lose their enabler or the enabler falls short, the Slob will sponge off someone else, whoever is handy.

Every community has Slobs, but not all Slobs are out committing crimes. Some Slobs work and hold down steady jobs. They find a niche in life. They slip occasionally and sometimes are irresponsible, but the employer has learned to be tolerant. A Slob will succeed on the job as long as the job is routine and does not require responsibility. They need to be told what to do and what is expected of them with the least amount of accountability or having to think for themselves. Slobs don't have to be criminals at all and most of them find a niche sooner or later by either finding someone to take care of them or falling into some kind of routine employment which is more a matter of luck than design. Those who don't work or freeload, by necessity, steal or deal, (there are no other choices), and sooner or later they get caught up in the criminal justice system and are made completely useless with no responsibilities at all.

SLOBS AND THE DO-GOODER

Do-gooders and Slobs don't mix. They are the worst of all combinations. The world is full of rescuers and that's not all bad.

When we become ill and must go to the hospital, we hope that the doctor on duty knows what he is doing and takes over the problem and rescues us from our illness. We hope the nurse on duty will take care of us. But that's different. Rescuers are necessary because we are in a vulnerable position and unable to be in charge of our life and solve our own problems.

The criminal justice system is full of rescuers who want to help criminals see the light. The problem is they run smack into criminal Slobs who absorb do-gooders like a dry sponge. Slobs love do-gooders. They rely on rescuers. But Slicks play games with them.

SLICKS AND THE DO-GOODER

A Slick named George was an ex-convict who always managed to get out of prison early. He had a formula that always worked.

Says George: "When you get to prison, the first thing you do is become an outrageous jerk. Be violent, be crazy, be spooky, be kinky, threaten suicide, upset the whole place. Let them send you to the psychiatric ward, but whatever you do, make sure everyone knows about you right up to the warden. Then, you lock onto a do-gooder and bare your soul to him. Tell him how miserable you are and then slowly but surely let the do-gooder rehabilitate you. Whatever his pet program is, buy into it. If it is religion, buy into religion. If it's alcohol treatment, be an alcoholic and let him treat you. In the end, change to what they want. Show great progress and when you go before the parole board, it will be plain for everyone to see that you are rehabilitated and the do-gooder will verify it's true. Then, it's out the door and back to the streets."

LADY, SOMEDAY YOU MIGHT THANK ME

A lady is traveling in her car alone at night down a long, lonely, country highway, trying to get home before a storm sets in. She is afraid. Suddenly she hears a loud bang and she discovers she has a flat tire. She pulls over along the shoulder of the road, gets out of the car and then begins to panic. She does not know how to change a tire. No one ever taught her how. After waiting for what seemed to be an eternity, in the distance she sees the lights of an approaching car. She is frightened. The car approaches and slows down and stops. A man rolls down his window.

"You got a problem, lady?"

"Yes, I have a flat tire."

"Do you know how to change a tire?"

"No, I've never learned how."

"Well, I'll help you."

The man proceeds to get out of his car, take off his jacket and dig in his own trunk. He then proceeds to jack up the lady's car, loosen the bolts, take off the flat tire and put on the lady's spare tire from her trunk. After about 15 minutes, she is ready to be on her way.

"Oh, I'm so glad you came along. I don't know what I would have done without you."

She offers to pay him some money; he refuses.

"Glad to help you. I hope you get home all right."

So he leaves. He feels happy. He rescued a poor damsel in distress.

She leaves. She's happy. What a nice man.

But she still doesn't know how to change a tire.

Let's go back and start the story all over again. The lady gets a flat tire and a man drives up and the following dialogue occurs:

"You got a problem, lady?"

"Yes, I have a flat tire."

"Do you know how to fix it?"

"No."

"Maybe you should learn."

"Yes, I guess I've never had to do it. There has always been someone around to do it for me."

"That may not always be the case. Someday you might be

caught out here like you are tonight and no one will come along. If a bad blizzard came along, you could freeze to death."

"Oh, that would be terrible."

"Certainly would. So, now's as good a time to learn as ever."

"But I'll get all dirty."

"So will I if I do it for you."

"Will you show me how," she asked.

"Sure, open your trunk."

"What do I do first?"

"What do you think?"

"I don't know."

"Well, think it through."

"I suppose I have to loosen those nuts on the wheel, is that right?"

"Try it and see."

"Which wrench do I use?"

"See what fits."

"Don't I have to jack the car up first?"

"I suppose."

"How do I do that?"

"Figure it out."

By this time the lady is getting angry.

"You know how to do it, why are you giving me such a hard time?" she glares at him.

"If I do it for you, you'll never learn how. Someday maybe you'll thank me."

The lady proceeded to jack up the car after much trial and error, getting herself dirty, snagging her nylons, breaking her fingernails, scraping her knuckles. She got the tire on. As she got into her car, she slammed the door and drove away, muttering to herself, "That jerk just stood there and watched me. I've never been so angry in all my life."

But she learned how to change a tire.

Chapter 7

PROBATION: A GREAT IDEA THAT DOESN'T WORK

Probation began in 1840 when a police officer asked a judge not to pack a young criminal away to prison, but, rather, to put the young lad on probation to the policeman and see if he could get the young man on the straight and narrow, an alternative to prison, a chance to go straight.

The whole concept should be abolished as an experiment that didn't work. First of all, it is a waste of talent. Most probation officers mean well and are, at least in the beginning, trying to do a good job. They work hard and they work long hours. They try but their job is thankless, frustrating and doomed before it starts. Their talents are wasted on menial paperwork and their talents should be redirected. Their job should not be eliminated but redirected so they can fulfill their potential instead of burning out. There is an old saying that a young probation officer goes through a cycle when dealing with criminals on probation. The first year he can't do enough for them. The second year he can't do enough to them and the third year he doesn't give a damn.

The answer is, probation officers are doomed before they start. The judge sets down the rules and turns losers over to the probation officer to monitor. An impossible task. What happens in the real world of the streets, probation turns out to be a big game that is impossible to make credible. Probation by its very conception creates a Parent-Child relationship. The probation officer and the courts are the Parent and the criminal is the Child who must live by the rules.

Slicks love to play "I'm smarter than you" and "Let's make a fool out of you." Probation with rules is a ready-made game for a Slick. A Slick will work overtime finding a way to play games with the rules. Slicks play life like a chessboard and a probation officer is just another piece on the board. The Slick's brain says: "Tell him what he wants to hear. I'll play him like a violin. Catch me if you can, sucker."

Probation officers usually fall into two categories: The hard line rear-end-kicker, who runs around trying to bust probationers for cheating on the rules, and soft rear-end-kissers, who run around trying to be friends to a bunch of losers. The sad thing about it is that it doesn't have to be that way at all. But it's not going to change unless the system changes and that will be discussed later.

Slicks are locked into a perpetual game of shortcutting and making a fool out of anybody who opposes them. A probation officer is an ideal set-up for a Slick. A probation officer may have many Slicks to deal with. A Slick can devote full time to "outsmarting" the probation officer. It's not a fair match at all.

One Federal study (the Government Accounting Office) revealed that 37% of those put on probation commit crimes while on probation and 45% commit crimes after discharge from probation. The study can only reflect what is discovered or admitted to. The average Slick is hard to tie down, they commit a lot of crime and sure as hell don't admit to anything. The study is probably accurate when interviewing Slobs. Slobs chirp like magpies about their stupid impulsive, nickel-dime pilfering. Slicks, when they chirp, are usually putting someone on and laughing about it later.

Probation is giving a criminal another chance to go straight. The fear of prison is supposed to shape them up. But Slicks look at everything as a game and probation is a perfect set-up for another game, a game the probation officer is bound to lose. Slicks shake the dice every time they commit a crime. It's part of the excitement. They know they flirt with prison every time they plan another crime. When they lose, they fully expect to pay the price. But even when they are caught, they still feel confident they can slick their way out of the jam. Probation is just another way of slicking themselves out of prison. In short, Slicks should go to prison. They should be removed from society, not only to protect society, but to give them what they gambled on beating. White-collar Slicks or street Slicks commit a lot of crimes. They're great believers in: "If you can't do the time, don't do the crime". Sappy but true. Why disappoint them?

Putting Slicks on probation is simply asking to make a fool out of the criminal justice system, yet judges do it every day because they can't tell a Slick when they've got one in front of their judicial noses.

But there are other criminals besides Slicks. The one type of criminal probation officers love is the winner who has a bad day and commits an out-of-character crime. In other words, a normally responsible person who commits an irresponsible act, something we all do on occasion but generally not serious enough to get us into the criminal justice system. Probably 80% or more of the youngsters who appear in juvenile court fit this description. They're nice to deal with. They lick the probation officer's hand like a cocker spaniel. They're polite, punctual and are wonderful on probation. They follow the rules and thank everyone for being so nice. They report on time and if ordered to pay restitution or perform community service, they not only do a good job, they do more than they are obligated to do. They make every pet correction program look good. Probation officers feel like a teacher with a class full of kids, all with their hands up, wanting to be called upon. They bend over backwards to prove they are good kids. They simply made a mistake and probably never will make the same mistake again. Probation officers all over the country probably spend more than half of their time on these cute cuddly little kids, but it's a complete waste of time and taxpayer's money.

They're not the problem.

Slobs and probation officers go around and around. They need each other. The critical, no-nonsense drill sergeant type of probation officer spends half his time chastizing, disciplining, browbeating and throwing his hands up in the air over Slobs. If you enjoy putting people down, there is nothing like badmouthing a Slob. They are perfect, made-to-order "Kick-mes". If one wants to be disappointed, lay responsibility on a Slob. Guaranteed. Tell them to meet you at three o'clock. They won't show. Why? They forgot. Their mother forgot to remind them. Their clock stopped. Someone forgot to mark it on the calendar. They thought it was tomorrow. It wasn't written down for them. They tried to call; no one answered. They forgot where the courthouse is.

If the probation officers happen to be "I only want to help you" rescuers, they are made-to-order for Slobs. And Slobs are made-to-order for them. Like St. Bernard dogs with casks of brandy around their necks, they will gravitate toward the Slobs who are caught up in the avalanche of life, waiting to be rescued.

Slobs do lousy on probation. Probation means they are supposed to act like responsible people...follow the rules...obey the laws...be productive...behave like normal people do. But Slobs are not responsible, normal people, so they fail miserably at being responsible. They have never known what responsibility is, so when a judge tells them to be responsible, it's meaningless. They are doomed before they start. Consequently, they violate probation and get kicked, wind up in the prison system, where they are completely taken care of, which is not all bad for a Slob.

A crusty old man approached a judge one day and said, "What's this probation stuff anyway? You tell a crook to go home and behave...Well, ain't that what everyone's supposed to do anyway? That's a nothing sentence if I ever heard of one." And he's right. It is a nothing sentence, but he's also wrong because the old man assumes that Slobs know what responsibility is, when they don't, and that they are capable of being normal responsible people.

SPARE ME FROM THE RESCUERS

There is a type of person who loves to go around giving advice and solving other people's problems. The Ann Landers-Dear Abby Syndrome. It seems these types of people often have problems of their own, deep down problems, but it's easier to go around meddling in other people's problems than dealing with their own, so they become do-good rescuers, advice-givers and people savers. And who better to focus their attention on than a sad sack, "poor me", "if only my prince will come" Slob.

Rescuers always get to feel good. Slobs are always appreciative as long as rescuers take over their problems. If you call them on their irresponsibility, they will snap and bite back and dump the guilt on you. "What have you ever done for me? I thought your job was to help me, all you do is lean on me." Slobs are good at dumping guilt trips on their critics. They've done it all their lives.

Many people who go into human service work go into people helping for what appears to be humanitarian reasons, but many go into people helping for their own needs as well. It always feels good to help the less fortunate. There are Sister Teresas and Dr. Albert Schweitzers in this world, people who give gold stamps without looking for trading stamps in return. But there are also many who want to help others to make themselves feel good in return, people who are like a cat that rubs up against your leg to pet itself...getting to use another to feel good, all under the guise of doing good. Most of the time it's harmless, but getting to feel good off a bunch of Slobs makes Slobs worse, not better, for it breeds irresponsibility.

CREATING ARTIFICIAL CRIMES

Probably the greatest criticism of probation is that it creates artificial crimes, crimes that are not crimes except in the world of corrections.

A young man named Clyde, who wasn't either a Slick or a Slob, was drinking too much. Normally Clyde was reasonably responsible, but one day while drinking with the boys he got irresponsible and wrote out a $35.00 worthless check to buy everyone some booze. The check bounced and Clyde wound up in court before a judge. The judge, after lecturing Clyde on the evils of drinking, ordered him to make the bad check good, which he did, but the judge went further and gave Clyde two years of prison but stayed the sentence and ordered Clyde to be on probation for two years. Thus, Clyde was ordered not to drink, which he kind of didn't, and to violate no laws, local, State or Federal, which he didn't, and to report to a probation officer every Thursday afternoon, which he did, for a while anyway. After a year of useless Thursday afternoon chatter, he decided it was a waste of time for everyone concerned and stopped showing up. A year passed by when suddenly the cops dropped by and picked up Clyde and dragged him before the same judge for violation of probation.

"I've been good," said Clyde.

"You failed to report to your probation officer as ordered," replied the angry judge.

"I felt it was a waste of everybody's time," replied Clyde.

"It's not for you to decide," said the judge as he ordered Clyde off to the state prison for two years.

Clyde went to prison, was a model prisoner, didn't bother anyone. After a year-and-a-half, he was placed on a release program at a work farm.

Clyde worked in the fields for a while and then got lonely for his girlfriend and one day got depressed and walked away.

Clyde married the lady and got a job as a hired hand on a farm, had his own mobile home and soon there were three kids, a dog, a cat and a TV satellite dish. He paid his taxes, quit drinking and sang in the church choir.

Then one day the law arrived and Clyde found himself looking up at the same judge. This time he was charged with prison escape and given 10 years.

"But I haven't done anything wrong," pleaded Clyde. "Ten years ago I wrote a bad check and paid it back. Since then I haven't taken a penny that has not belonged to me, nor have I hurt a hair on another person's body. I've been a law-abiding citizen. I can't believe this is happening to me."

The judge was unmoved. Clyde was convicted. He had no legal defense and was sent off to the state prison for ten years.

"Maybe you haven't hurt anyone, but you violated our rules," said the judge. "We must make an example of you, otherwise others may think they can walk away from our institutions also." (The judge apparently believed that losers have conventions and discuss things like that.)

A farfetched story? Not at all. Our prisons are full of people who are there because they violated the rules rather than commit new crimes.

In Clyde's case, society paid tens of thousands of dollars to prove nothing. His wife and children went on welfare and instead of paying taxes and being a productive citizen, he and his family became dependents of society. A total net loss.

What went wrong? The judge should have ordered Clyde to pay back four times what he had wrongfully taken. (Moses' rule.) Once paid, the matter should have been forgotten; and if he wrote another check, then four times the amount again until Clyde figured out that writing bum checks can be expensive. But the judge got Clyde wrapped up in the game of probation and all its

"Maybe you didn't hurt anyone or steal anything...BUT, YOU VIOLATED OUR RULES!!"

rules. Sure, in retrospect Clyde should have reported every Thursday and he shouldn't have walked away from the work farm, but he harmed no one except the dignity of the rule-makers, and society and his family in the long run paid the price.

In conclusion, probation doesn't work very well. It is impossible to make probation credible. Losers all over the country on probation are violating the terms of their probation everyday and getting away with it. It makes the justice system look like a bunch of foolish games. Games Slicks love to play without any encouragement whatsoever. It's a disaster with Slicks.

For Slobs, it is simply setting them up to lose, which they will more often than not, and to entangle them ever further in the system until they become hopelessly institutionalized in stagnation and total dependence.

Does that mean that probation officers do more harm than good? No. We need these people, but we must change their roles. We must make them a vital part of the sentencing process instead of charging them with meaningless responsibilities and duties that take up their time, their enthusiasm and energy. They must become sentencing specialists in human behavior and learn the techniques of confronting Slicks and Slobs so that they can help criminals change their erroneous reasoning and thought patterns, a much more challenging career than what corrections officers now face...an impossible task that can only lead to burnout.

People who believe in probation get very angry when probation is criticized, and that's understandable. No one likes to hear that maybe what one earns their living at is futile and non-productive. The problem is their profession is controlled directly by the judge's sentences, and if the judge's sentences make no sense, then what is followed up by the probation officer makes no sense either. The blind leading the blind. Like the colonial doctor, good intentions, lousy theory.

Chapter 8

SOLUTIONS

Previous chapters have described the problems posed by the Slicks and Slobs in our society. The role of the criminal justice system in compounding these problems has also been covered. But where do little Slicks and Slobs come from? How do we save our tax dollars and empty our jails by out-slicking Slicks and de-slobbing Slobs?

Winners and losers are created at an early age, labels are attached to the winners and losers in our midst. By the time they reach an age where they can be accomodated by the criminal justice system, Slicks and Slobs are generally quite comfortable in their roles. In handling Slicks and Slobs it is crucial for practitioners in the justice system to first recognize these character disorders. Next, judges must impose responsible sentences that make the Slick and Slob uncomfortable enough to want to change. Finally, the status quo must be restored, the victim must be made whole, the damages repaired or paid for. The Slick or Slob must be required to own the problem, to restore the status quo, no one else can own the problem.

CONFRONTING SLICKS AND SLOBS

Rule of Thumb No. 1: There are winners and losers and both wind up in court. Winners take care of themselves, take charge of their lives in a responsible manner and the sentence they receive is of little consequence. The sentence should be responsible, constructive and beneficial to society, as well as the offender. A great number of offenders fall into this category.

Rule of Thumb No. 2: Violent people should be locked up to protect society. Murderers, rapists, child molesters and brutal people have forfeited their right to be free. Very few offenders fall into this category. The criminally insane must be, for the same reason, confined.

Rule of Thumb No. 3: Slicks should be locked up. They commit a lot of crime for high stakes. Society must be protected. While incarcerated, they must be confronted to look at their thought and reasoning processes and to be de-slicked. But anyone who works with a Slick must be as slick as the Slick or they will be out-slicked in the process. Fortunately, very few offenders are Slicks.

Rule of Thumb No. 4: Slobs must be made responsible, to take charge of their lives and to own their problems. Slobs don't have to be Slobs. They can become productive members of our society. Our criminal justice system is cram-packed with them. They are clogging our courts to the point of breaking them down. The traditional methods used in the past have been more harmful than helpful. We unwittingly have been making worse Slobs out of our Slobs, simply because we have failed to understand them or their thought patterns. Corrections workers should be spending 90% of their time understanding and confronting Slobs instead of packing them away or spending their time on responsible people who made an out-of-character mistake, winners who committed a losing act. Slobs are losers who continue to commit losing acts over and over again until they change themselves.

Rule of Thumb No. 5: Treat Slobs like responsible adults, not like irresponsible children. Parent-Child confrontations bring out the worst in a Slob. Corrections workers who always come off in a parental way should join the police force, the military service or become football referees. Corrections workers who always come off as the rescuing nurturing parent should become doctors, nurses, firemen, social workers or ambulance drivers and leave the Slobs alone.

Rule of Thumb No. 6: Put the problem on the Slob who has the problem. Make Slobs own their problems. If they refuse to own their problems, make life so uncomfortable that they will rescue themselves. Stress and uncertainty cause anxiety, which causes motivation to change. As long as a Slob is comfortable, there will be no change.

Rule of Thumb No. 7: Move offenders in and out of the criminal justice system as fast as possible. Winners will get back on the winning track immediately. They will be gone and seen no more. Slicks should be tried as rapidly as possible and if convicted, sent straight to jail. Do the crime, do the time. Slobs should be forced to be immediately responsible to their victims, the community and themselves. The sooner they become responsible, the sooner they are free, but they must earn their way out, no excuses, dragging their heels or rescuing allowed.

Rule of Thumb No. 8: Slobs are faced with the same four choices in life that everyone else has. They must find a niche in life. In other words, if they can't become employable, they must find a host to freeload from. If they can't work or freeload, they will, by necessity, be stealing or dealing again and continue to be caught up in the criminal justice system.

Rule of Thumb No. 9: Don't rescue Slobs. Show them you care about them, that you want them to live a happy responsible life, but under no condition will you own or take over their problem.

Rule of Thumb No. 10: Criticize a Slob's acts and his behavior but never degrade, put down or destroy what little self-worth a Slob has left. Hate the act but never the person. Remember, all Slobs can change. They have the ability to be responsible if they want to, but change must come from within and changing the self-image is the key to responsibility.

THE ELEMENTS OF A RESPONSIBLE RESTITUTION SENTENCE

1. Community involvement or self-help.
2. Restitution to the community.
3. Comunity involvement or self-help.
4. Time necessary to complete sentence.
5. Penalty for failure.
6. Verification by offender.

RESPONSIBLE SENTENCES

John is an unemployed nineteen-year-old who is in jail for burglary. He broke into a manufacturing plant and pried open a pop machine in search of money. The police saw a shadow moving around inside the building. They found a broken window, surrounded the place and found John hiding in a closet. John confessed to the crime, pled guilty to burglary and the judge referred him to a Court Service officer to arrive at a sentence that made sense.

John wasn't in an ordinary court. He was fortunate to have Judge Weaver as the sentencing Judge. Weaver was a new breed, a judge who broke away from traditional sentencing methods and believed that courts should make offenders responsible for their crimes rather than useless dependents.

Working in conjunction with Judge Weaver was a young Court Service officer named Patty. She was called a Court Service officer because Judge Weaver had abolished forever the concept of probation. It was an unspeakable word. When anyone, including the offender, said "probation", they received a strange puzzled look that meant "what's that?"

Patty could read a Slick or a Slob moments after meeting them. She met John, read the police report and began her interview with him.

Patty: What did you do, John?
John: They say burglary.
Patty: What do you say?
John: I guess so.
Patty: You did it, didn't you?
John: Ya.
Patty: Why?
John: Stupid, I guess.
Patty: What were you after?
John: Some cash to buy booze.
Patty: Aren't you working?
John: No.
Patty: How come?
John: Jobs are hard to find.
Patty: You got any skills?
John: Naw.

Patty: Why not?
John: I don't know.
Patty: Quit school?
John: Yah.
Patty: How you surviving?
John: I get along.
Patty: Well, who you freeloading off?
John: No one. I get along.
Patty: Who you trying to fool? If you're not working or freeloading, you're stealing or dealing, no other choice.
John: Naw, not me.
Patty: Must be the tooth fairy who is supporting you, John.
John: Naw.
Patty: How come you have to get along for another day by ripping someone off?
John: Lousy luck. I guess I need a job.
Patty: Sitting in jail doesn't help much.
John: What's this judge going to do to me?
Patty: That's up to you.
John: What do you mean?
Patty: It's responsibility time.
John: I suppose.
Patty: You can sit in a slammer and be useless or you can start being responsible. It's your problem.
John: Well, what should I do?
Patty: I don't know, it's your problem.
John: But isn't it your job to tell me what to do?
Patty: Nope, I just sit around and listen to your excuses.
John: Well, what am I here for?
Patty: To get responsible.
John: Okay, I'll get responsible, whatever that means.
Patty: You want to sit in jail?
John: No, I can't stand the place. Last time I nearly lost it.
Patty: Live an irresponsible life and you'll see a lot of jails. What are you going to tell the judge next time you're in front of him for sentencing?
John: I'll tell him I'll be good.
Patty: That will impress him. He's never heard that before.
John: Well, what should I tell him?
Patty: I don't know. I'm not the burglar, you are. It's your

rear end that's going to get locked up, not mine.
John: I'll ask for probation.
Patty: He doesn't know what that means.
John: Well, I was drunk. That's why I broke into that building.
Patty: I've been drunk, too, but I sure didn't break into any buildings. Quit making excuses. Why don't you start looking at who you have wronged and start making it right?
John: You mean paying for the damages?
Patty: That's good for starters.
John: How much were the damages?
Patty: How should I know. It's your problem.
John: Will you find out what the damages are?
Patty: Nope.
John: Why not?
Patty: It's your problem; call them up.
John: I suppose I could. What if they get angry at me?
Patty: That's the chance you take when you rip people off.
John: If I offer to pay for the window and the damaged pop machine, do you think the judge will go light on me?
Patty: I don't know. If you wind up in prison, you guessed wrong.
John: Well, what more can I do?
Patty: What do you think? You ever thought of over paying the damages to make up for the inconvenience you've caused that company?
John: I suppose I could do that, but I don't have a job.
Patty: Then get one.
John: How?
Patty: Like everyone else does. We've had kids, juveniles, who have shoveled sidewalks, mowed lawns, cut firewood and all kinds of things like that. If they can do it, so can you.
John: Naw, that's kid stuff. I don't want to do that.
Patty: Then sit in jail.
John: Can't you find me a decent job?
Patty: Why should I? I've got a job. You get one for yourself. That's the problem, you want someone to rescue you. Life's not that way.

John: You can talk smart. You've got a job, nice office, good pay.
Patty: I didn't get here by getting drunk and burglarizing pop machines. Quit playing "poor me". You've got nobody to blame but yourself. There's nothing wrong with you. Quit feeling sorry for yourself.
John: Well, I don't like myself very well. I never have.
Patty: You are what you think you are. If you keep seeing yourself as a loser, then you'll be a loser. Only you can change that.
John: I wish I could.
Patty: We've got a program that gives you all kinds of ideas on how to change, if you want to. It meets three nights a week. Want to join?
John: Naw, that's kid stuff.
Patty: I suppose ripping off pop machines is grown-up, macho stuff.
John: I suppose not. Do you suppose the judge will go for it if I tell him I want to join your program?
Patty: Won't hurt to try. How about your boozing? You got a problem?
John: Naw. It's no problem.
Patty: Then why are you in jail? You got drunk and pulled a second-rate nickel-dime burglary and ended up in jail. That's not a problem?
John: I suppose it is. I figure I drink because I feel so lousy about everything. If only I had a job, I'd feel better and quit drinking.
Patty: Quit playing "if only". "If only this" or "if only that", that's how irresponsible people think. You can sit and wait for "if only" the rest of your life. Nobody's going to rescue you except yourself. Boozing is part of losing if it takes over your life.
John: You think I should see somebody about my drinking?
Patty: That's up to you, it's your problem.
John: Well, I think I will. I'm getting a little sick of all the hassles I get into and it seems to happen every time I drink too much.
Patty: Who do you hang around with?
John: Oh, I drink with the boys down at the Riverside Bar.
Patty: Costs money to drink. Who's your enabler?

John: My what?
Patty: Your enabler. When you don't support yourself, someone else has to pick up the slack. Someone who carries you for another day, another day of irresponsibility, they are what we call an enabler. They enable you to be irresponsible and as long as the enabler keeps enabling, you'll keep right on being irresponsible.
John: Well, my mother gives me a few bucks.
Patty: Then she's your enabler and she better get involved with your problem so she can realize that enablers create and perpetuate irresponsibility.
John: I never thought about that. She does it because she feels sorry for me. Loves me, I guess.
Patty: Sounds like she's killing you with kindness. Don't you do anything except hang around the Riverside Bar?
John: Not really, nothing much else to do.
Patty: Why don't you join the world instead of sitting on the sidelines like a spectator?
John: I'm not a joiner.
Patty: What else do you do besides slopping beer and playing pool at the Riverside?
John: I like to hunt and fish.
Patty: Ever thought about joining the Valley Sportsmen's Club? They are real active in wildlife and saving the environment.
John: I don't think they'd want me.
Patty: You'll never know until you ask them.
John: Well, what's this got to do with what I'm going to have to tell the judge?
Patty: Maybe nothing, maybe a lot. The judge likes people to put something back into this world to make up for ripping it off.
John: You mean if I join the Sportsmen's Club and promise to work on their wildlife projects, the judge will go light on me?
Patty: It's not that simple. He'll tell you that promises never feed a bulldog. He wants deeds, honest-to-goodness work or it's back to the slammer. In Judge Weaver's court you have to propose the sentence to him. You have to tell him what you are going to do to get out and stay out of jail. It's up to you. No probation, no

rules, nobody watching you, no reporting to me, none of that Mickey Mouse mentality. You've got to put up or be locked up, and you've got to prove you've done it. I won't play shepherd over you for a minute. It's your responsibility, your problem, not mine. Anytime you want to drop by and talk to me, that's fine, I'm here, but don't be looking for me to hold your hand. I don't nursemaid anybody. It's not my problem and not my job.

John: How are you going to know I'm living up to my end of the bargain?

Patty: That's your problem. There is going to be a time limit on getting things done and you have to prove it to us and if you don't, it's back to jail. And even your jail time is going to be agreed-upon before you leave court. You're even going to have to come up with how much time you are going to sit if you don't live up to your promise. That way everything is tied down so you'll know at all times what your penalty will be if you fail.

John: What if I tell the judge I'll only go to jail for a day if I goof up?

Patty: Then he probably won't buy your deal and you'll stay in jail. He's not stupid, you know.

John: You mean I can negotiate?

Patty: Sure, but if you don't come up with a responsible built-in penalty, you'll be sitting a long time. So, don't play games with Judge Weaver.

John: Well, I'll be darned. What should I tell him?

Patty: Hey, that's your problem.

John: You mean everything's up to me?

Patty: That's right. It's called responsibility, taking charge of your life and owning your problems. The ball is in your court.

With that, Patty and John spend another two hours discussing and putting together a responsible proposal that John would make to the judge. John decided that he would pay the victim for all the damages that occurred for the break-in, that he would raise the money himself (legally) and not borrow the money from his parents, that he would pay an additional $100.00 to the victims for their inconvenience and bother that resulted from his crime. If he was unable to raise the money, he would contribute free work at the rate of minimum wages per hour to the victim's company doing maintenance, clean-up work or whatever they desired. John called and Patty arranged for a meeting with the plant manager and John at the jail. The plant manager agreed to John's proposal.

Patty knew John was a Slob, that his problem was irresponsibility. John agreed to join her three nights a week in a self-image changing course. John also agreed to join the Valley Sportsmen's Club and donate 80 hours of work to wildlife projects, cleaning up game refuges and the environment. He also agreed to join group sessions with an alcohol counselor that met twice a week. John made all the arrangements over the telephone from the jailhouse without any help from Patty. (She did break down and loan him a Telephone Directory.) John also agreed to get a job, any kind of a job, or go back to jail.

For the penalty provision for failure to perform, John agreed to do 90 days in jail. But John assured Patty that he would perform. He didn't like jail at all.

Everything was put down in writing and signed by John. A couple days later John and Patty went into court with their proposal. John wanted Patty to speak for him. She refused. (It's your problem.)

John stood up in court and told Judge Weaver his proposal. He submitted his written agreement. The judge studied it and accepted the proposal. John was set free immediately. His agreement had to be completed within 90 days or it was back to jail. It was his responsibility to prove compliance by filing written receipts and verification with Patty before the 90 days were up. He knew if he failed he would be jailed for 90 days thereafter.

John got a job cleaning septic tanks (a job he had turned down before). He paid the manufacturing plant for the damages plus $100.00. He completed 80 hours of volunteer work restoring wildlife habitat and attended all the required alcohol counseling sessions. Most important of all, he took part in Patty's self-image program* and became acutely aware for the first time in his life what responsibility is. John was discharged from the court system after 90 days and began functioning as a normal citizen in our society. John still is a non-winner, but at least he isn't a hopeless

---

*The Pacific Institute, Inc., 100 W. Harrison Plaza, Seattle, WA 98119 has developed a 'Changing Directions' program to develop self-esteem. This program shows great promise.

loser. But he's trying. At least the system didn't make him worse.

There are millions of Johns across America. Unfortunately, most of them are sitting in jails or prisons doing pointless, endless time freeloading off society. The cycle must be broken.

THE GENESIS OF A SLOB

Slobs don't have to be Slobs. They are not born that way, they are created. It starts at the kitchen table, nurtured by the school system and finished off by the criminal justice system.

Let's look at John. As long as he could remember, he could never do anything right. His father, when he was around, was a critical tyrant who took out his own losing frustrations on John. Constantly being critical of the boy, the boy soon did nothing. It seemed nothing was the easy way out because if he attempted to do anything, it didn't turn out and his father would punish him. His mother, although dominated by the father, usually rescued poor John and came to his defense. John was caught, as most Slobs are, between a persecuting, degrading, critical parent and a rescuing, nurturing parent.

One day when John was four years old, he decided to draw a cat. He started with his crayons and soon he drew a purple cat. At least to his way of thinking it was a cat. He decided to show his mother the cat. Mother was busy cooking dinner when John showed her the cat. Being busy and late, she was irritable and looked at John's cat, ignored it, and went on with her chores. John felt bad. "She doesn't like my cat," John thought, "I'll draw a better one." So, he started all over again. This time he worked harder and longer on the drawing. When it was finished, his older sister came through the door. John ran up to her and proudly showed her his drawing. She looked at it, "Looks like a rat to me," and walked away. John looked at the picture. "That's not a rat, it's a cat." Saddened and disappointed, John returned to his paper pad and started all over again. This time he would draw the perfect cat, a beautiful cat for everyone to see. After an hour, he triumphantly produced the finished drawing. Dad came through the door,

"Look at my cat, dad." Dad looked at it and said, "That's a cat? Boy, you'll never make an artist," and walked away.

And there went tomorrow's Norman Rockwell.

John hung around the playground. He watched other kids playing softball and wanted to play but was afraid to ask. One day he asked if he could play and they reluctantly let him. He was picked last. John was nervous and struck out every time he was at bat. The next day neither side picked him. One day when there weren't enough kids to make up two teams, they looked at John. One kid shook his head, "He strikes out all the time, we'd be better off without him." John said he wouldn't strike out this time, so they let him play. John struck out.

There went tomorrow's Pete Rose.

When John went to school, he liked music class. One day the teacher asked the class to sing a song that had a chorus. When the song got around to the chorus, she would point at one of the children and that child would sing the chorus. After a few verses she pointed to John. He was so glad she called on him he sang loud and clear...but he mixed up a word and got flustered, sang off key and the class laughed. John was humiliated.

There went tomorrow's John Denver.

These events or similar ones occur in everyone's childhood, but multiply these events by a thousand and you can understand why John soon judged himself to be a loser. His mother made things worse. She failed to raise his self-esteem, began to feel sorry for John and started making excuses for him, taking over his problems and rescuing him. Unfortunately, John let her. He became a dormant, passive loser, a left-behind Slob.

Undoing eighteen years of losing is not an easy task. But there was nothing wrong with John. He has the same potential as anyone else, except John doesn't think so. He sees himself as a loser. Inadequate, frustrated and unhappy, he lets other people make a loser out of him and, worse yet, he compounds the problem by telling himself he is a loser.

Slobs learn in life that if you get into a jam, people will rescue you and take over the problem. They become parasites by living off others. They let others be responsible for them and they get along for another day.

What a Slob needs is a success in his life, any success, a small success, just something to reverse his low self-esteem and losing ways.

Degrading them, making a fool out of them is devastating and makes things worse, yet our criminal justice system does everything in its official capacity to do just that.

Liberals (Corrections Liberals, not Democrats) created some programs intended to rehabilitate losers. Group sessions, one-on-one confrontations, half-way houses, group homes and work release were all positive steps in the right direction, but they failed to have insight into what Slobs were all about and, worse yet, they mixed Slicks into their programs, which is a recipe for utter disaster.

DE-SLOBBING A SLOB

Recent criminal studies proclaim there is evidence that criminals are of lower than average intelligence and they may be genetically different. Once again, these researchers are college professor types who lump all criminals together so their research is flawed from the start. Slicks are smarter than average. They have to be. A Slick can't play "I'm smarter than you" and "let's make a fool out of the justice system" by having below normal intelligence. Slobs on the other hand tend to be, on the average, less intelligent for the simple reason that low self-esteem plays a dominant role. People who are less intelligent or mentally handicapped have good reason to feel inadequate. They are less adequate if they don't work harder to overcome the deficit. It is easy for them to default and give up and become a dropout in the rat race of life. In short, a person who has lower intelligence has a greater potential of being a Slob and a large percentage of criminals are Slobs.

First of all, Slobs must want to change. No amount of kicking is going to make them want to change, particularly when our system takes over their lives and in essence makes them comfortable dependents. For the average person, jail is not comfort, nor is it even conceivable that it could be, but for Slobs it's just another unlucky day in a miserable, unlucky life. Freedom to a winner is precious. To a loser, freedom means responsibility and responsibility means stress...something to avoid.

If a Slob is comfortable, he'll never change. Comfort to a Slob is the bare minimum. A place to stay, a roof over the head, something to eat and a place to hang out with other Slobs. (Slobs gravitate to other Slobs, they are part of each other's comfort zones.) Once he's in the holding pattern, a Slob can continue indefinitely. The problem is he can't remain in this rut without an enabler, someone to pay for the roof over the head and the food on the table. Parents, friends, the government. If the enabler's support is adequate, the Slob will remain relatively crime free. When the support system breaks down, the Slob, by necessity, resorts to petty theft or nickel-dime dealing. That's when he gets caught up in the justice system. Their crimes are unsophisticated, poorly planned, obvious and often committed while semi-drunk. Slobs are easily caught. Their crimes are quickly solved. The worst that can happen to them is they'll be taken care of by society. If they get away with the crime, they survive for another day. If they are caught and incarcerated, they survive for another day. By a loser's standards, they "win" either way.

Slobs must be confronted with the fact that they are irresponsible. This is a hard concept for them to understand, for being responsible is not part of their history of experiences. To them, it's just a matter of lousy luck. The "right break" that others always get just never seems to come along in their lives.

Their enabling system must be pointed out and removed. As long as the enablers are present, things will not change. Enablers are hard to remove. Slobs can get violent when their security is threatened. If aggression doesn't work, they resort to "hang dog", "poor me", "I'll commit suicide" tactics to make the rescuers feel sorry for them. Another problem with enablers is they oftentimes need a Slob around in order to feel needed. Removing the enabler causes a Slob great discomfort. There is a risk here as they must either become responsible for their lives or turn to crime. But the risk must be taken.

A Slob feels inferior. He must be convinced, which is hard to do, that the rest of the world often feels like he does: inadequate.

He must be made to realize he is a dependent type of person and must learn to stand on his own two feet instead of leaning on someone else. He must give up his "helpless" games that cause others to rescue him. His "helpless" games must be pointed out to him because he doesn't recognize the game he is in. To him it's normal.

Slobs desperately need employment, but employment is hard to come by because Slobs lack employable characteristics such as punctuality, trustworthiness, motivation, dependability, self-confidence, responsibility and usually good appearance.

Slobs do not make good job applicants. They lack confidence and show it. They are easily passed over.

Employers of Slobs must be tolerant and willing to put up with some losing characteristics. Once a Slob finds such an employer, he can start to support himself. If not fired, Slobs can find a niche in life and remain relatively crime free. If they can find a spouse who will take over money management and make responsible decisions, a Slob will make it from day to day without slipping back into crime.

Slobs need symbiotic relationships. They find it stressful to go it alone. So, the key to "habilitating" (not rehabilitating) or "responsibilizing" a Slob is to find them a healthy symbiotic relationship where they must be productive in order to maintain a relationship.

Making a Slob uncomfortable is the only way there is any hope for them to get off their dead rear ends and take charge of their lives. Many Slobs prefer jail to being responsible. To them, jail is easier and offers less stress. They don't like jail, will do whatever they can to avoid it; but if they land there, they'll endure it. They'll do their time. People will endure just about anything, but uncertainty drives them up a wall. Anyone working with Slobs must learn how to make them uncomfortable by putting the problem on the Slob who has the problem. The Slob is caught between doing absolutely nothing and taking the ultimate punishment or trying to work his way out of the stressful predicament.

Slobs can't stand success. With success always comes responsibility. Subconsciously or even consciously, a Slob knows that responsibility will be taken from them if they fail or screw up. This must be pointed out before they even start trying to be responsible. When a Slob screws up, the natural response is to take away his responsibilities, but in a Slob's world this amounts to a reward.

Slobs have had very few successes in their life and one must be patient. They expect failure. For every two steps forward, they fall back one. When they fail, there must be consequences, short and to the point, but consequences; and, if possible, the problem should be the consequence. For example: A Slob fails to do community service, so he is jailed. He should be then given the chance to work out of the jail during daytime hours to finish the job. When he finishes the work, he is rewarded by being released before his time is up. If, while he is in jail he carves his initials in the wall, he can either sand it off and repaint the wall or sit it out. If he repairs the damage, he is set free. Simple formula. Screw up requires immediate consequence, requires responsibility, equals reward. Most correction systems call for screw up equals punishment...end of story.

Slobs have developed by natural osmosis the ability to make up excuses for their irresponsibility. They must be challenged every time they try to peddle excuses. No excuses allowed. Only calls from the emergency ward of a hospital or the undertaker will be considered. All other excuses are ignored as just another gimmick to cover up irresponsibility. Slobs get very adept at excuse-making: My watch stopped...my mother didn't wake me...my grandmother was sick...the note you gave me was eaten up by a big dog...I couldn't get a ride...I forgot...and so forth. Slobs have learned that excuses will get you by, at least they have in the past. If one buys into a Slob's excuse, the Slob gets by for another day. The key is to anticipate the excuses in advance and point out that they won't be accepted. This causes the Slob stress, otherwise they feel they will always be given another chance. After all, it's always been that way in the past.

Slobs must be shown (once the enablers have been neutralized) that there are no tooth-fairies in this world, that rescuers on white horses don't exist and that sitting around waiting for them is a waste of time, that no one is going to save them except themselves; and thinking thoughts of "if only" is self-deception.

Risk taking in a positive direction is not part of a Slob's personality. They remain dormant and maintain the status quo. Like a traveler who must cross a river by stepping on the rocks, the Slob, once he's on a dry rock, wants to stay there. They do not like to risk new things because every time they have tried to do something in the past it ended in failure. Failure hurts, so the Slob doesn't try. That way they don't get hurt. Thus, they build mental cages that trap them into stagnation.

A dominant characteristic of a Slob is to make the same mistake over and over. To normal people, that's stupidity, but to a Slob it's bad luck. Slobs must be shown that when you go about being irresponsible, you're going to attract attention. Irresponsibility causes authoritarians to come into your life and authoritarians always kick rear ends...always have, always will. Accident prone people are not unlucky, they simply live a life that gets them into trouble. Slobs are poor probability estimators. Most of us have good probability estimation as to the success or failure of the decisions we make. We inherently realize that when we are faced with tough decisions, there are risks that are acceptable and risks that are foolhardy and long shots. Slobs always bet on the wrong horse. They seem to have a knack for making decisions that have little chance for success. They then blame bad luck and climb further back in their mental cage. "I tried...see what happened."

Alcohol, drugs and Slobs go together. Chemical abuse is part of their irresponsible behavior. When one feels lousy about life, one might as well get high. At least you can feel momentarily good, forget tomorrow. But we can't be deceived into blaming booze for the Slob's irresponsibility. A Slob is irresponsible whether he is drunk or not. It's just added baggage, that's all. Slobs should never be given the luxury of being able to blame alcohol or drugs for their irresponsible life.

Slobs often are deceptive at first glance. Some Slobs maintain phoney fronts. They don't like themselves and take on a tough guy image, trying to be something or someone they aren't. It's a way of gaining respect. If no one respects you in a positive way, then maybe they will respect you out of fear. That's why Slobs get beat up a lot and they go back for more. Macho Slobs go from bar to bar being the tough guy, holding themselves out for the inevitable thrashing they'll get sooner or later. It's the "kick me" mentality carried to an extreme.

Macho Slobs must be confronted with the fact that they are trying to gain respect in a losing way. People who project themselves as mean-looking dudes gain respect, but only negative respect.

A whole book can be and should be written on dealing with Slob mentality. But deal with them we must. Our over-crowded corrections system is bogged down with them. We need people who can develop skills to cope with them and make them responsible instead of contributing to their further irresponsibility. It is the challenge for corrections workers and criminal court judges of tomorrow. What we are doing today is disaster that is compounding disaster. In fact, it amounts to irresponsibility on our part.

OUT-SLICKING SLICKS

Simon was a Slick. Even his friends called him Sly. Considered cool, Sly was a high school dropout who was too smart for the teachers. "Those boring fools don't know nothing," said Simon as he held audience on the street corner with a group of local Slobs who nodded their heads in approval. Sly always had a problem with honesty. Anything he wanted was his God-given right to possess. He always figured he was one step ahead of the rest of the stupid human race. His parents were stupid, the teachers were stupid, the cops were stupid. People who worked hard at stupid jobs were stupid. He always figured he would make a good lawyer, he could talk his way out of anything, and he did, most of the time. Sly carried around a lot of anger. He felt people didn't give him the respect he deserved. The respect he deserved was also God-given, not earned. Sly was a ladies' man, able to seduce any woman he desired. He was considered handsome and had a charming personality when he wanted to turn it on. Often suspected by the police and often questioned, he gave them the "who me" smile and denied ever being involved in anything illegal. He liked detectives and often talked with them on the street corners. He admired lawyers. "They know how to get around things," said Sly. He could be a lawyer but he didn't want to waste all that time getting a degree.

One night Sly got busted for selling cocaine to an undercover agent. He was furious. "Sleazy narc, I'll get that creep if it's the last thing I do. I don't get angry, (he was), I get even." (Not original.) He immediately hired the best criminal lawyer in town, paid him in cash, up front. Where did he get it? "Borrowed it from a friend," smiled Sly. Sly and his lawyer put the prosecutor through the hoops. Give no quarter, ask no quarter. "Sly's constitutional rights were violated," cried his lawyer, "He was entrapped." He was tried and convicted by a jury of 12. Judge Weaver knew he had a Slick on his hands but referred Sly to his court service officer, Patty, to have her independent opinion. The following interview took place:

Sly: What's this all about?
Patty: A sentence recommendation conference.
Sly: This is a kangaroo court.

Patty: Why is that?
Sly: That sleazy narc violated my constitutional rights.
Patty: Is that right?
Sly: Yeah, I was entrapped.
Patty: Apparently the judge didn't think so.
Sly: Aw, he and the cops are all in cahoots.
Patty: If he ruled for you, I suppose he'd be in cahoots with you.
Sly: What are you, an expert?
Patty: No, everybody's stupid according to you.
Sly: That's right. Someday I'll teach you all not to violate my rights.
Patty: Well, did you do what they said you did?
Sly: What has that got to do with anything?
Patty: You sound like a Slick to me.
Sly: What's that?
Patty: People who play by their own rules but who get real indignant if someone else doesn't play by the rules.
Sly: Don't give me that garbage. They are supposed to be the high and mighty, the good guys, the upholders of the law. What a joke.
Patty: See what you want to see, but you're a game player to me.
Sly: What's that supposed to mean?
Patty: People who play life like a chess game, always looking for an angle...shortcutting...where can I get it wholesale...who can I screw over today?
Sly: Don't give me any of that Sunday School garbage.
Patty: Slicks don't like looking at themselves...the whole world is screwed up but them. How do you get along anyway? What keeps you afloat?
Sly: I get along.
Patty: You working?
Sly: Naw.
Patty: Got a girlfriend?
Sly: Lots of them. You should be so lucky.
Patty: Slicks make poor friends. Who is supporting you anyway?
Sly: No one.
Patty: Then you're stealing or dealing.
Sly: No, none of that.

Patty: Oh, the tooth fairy leaves money under your pillow every morning.
Sly: Aw, get lost.
Patty: It's your problem, not mine.
Sly: I don't have to talk to you.
Patty: No, you don't...you don't have any problems...none that you will own and deal with. What are you going to tell the judge at sentencing time?
Sly: Aw, I'll get probation. This is my first offense.
Patty: The first time you got caught.
Sly: They've got nothing on me other than this bum rap.
Patty: There is no probation in Judge Weaver's court. It's a restitution sentence or a prison sentence.
Sly: They can't lock me up on a first offense.
Patty: Why not?
Sly: I thought Judge Weaver didn't believe in prison.
Patty: For Slicks he does.
Sly: Who the hell says I'm a Slick? I'm just a guy who happened to get caught. There are people out there every day getting away with a lot of garbage worse than I did. Why don't they bust all the crooked businessmen in town? I'll tell you what I'll do, I'll cooperate with the police and tell you all kinds of things they would like to hear. I could help them solve a bunch of cases.
Patty: It's not my problem, but you sure go from one game to another. You're really moving your chess pieces now.
Sly: I could help them nail the real higher-up guys, but I'm not going to cooperate one crummy bit unless I get probation.
Patty: Now you're playing trading stamps, just another game. You're a compulsive manipulator. If you got probation you'd laugh your way out of the courtroom and you'd be playing a new game on the streets as soon as the neon lights came on. You're going to be caught up in the system for the rest of your life unless you face the fact that you're a game player who uses people to survive for another day. You're non-productive. You live by your wits, surviving by being slick, taking what other people work to produce. And everytime you do it you laugh at the stupid sucker you ripped off. Until you can see yourself for what you are, you are a hopeless case. All you're doing is winning at losing.

Sly went before Judge Weaver and he and his lawyer pleaded for probation. The judge refused and sent Sly off to the state prison. "You'll gain nothing in prison except how to be slicker at being slick," said the judge. But at least you'll be off the streets and there are plenty of young Slicks ready to move up to fill the vacancy. Your only hope is to change yourself. I understand the Department of Corrections is going to start a program for Slicks.* I hope you will join.

Sly was led away by a jailer. He turned to his lawyer and said, "What the hell is a Slick?" The lawyer shrugged his shoulders, "Beats me."

DE-SLICKING A SLICK

A Slick thinks he's fine, it's just the rest of the world that's screwed up. Until they realize that their thought pattern and reasoning are different, there is no hope for change. They will continue to rip off the world, get away with it most of the time, get caught, try to get out of the jam, and, if incarcerated, will set out to run and manipulate the prison. It is said that prisons in America are run by the inmates under an unspoken truce. If that is true then prisons are run by Slicks, not Slobs.

---

*The Minnesota Department of Corrections, during the 1970s, ran a program called Asklepieion. The Director, Dale Irestone, former inmate and an ex-Slick, ran a group confrontational therapeutic community within the walls of the Stillwater Prison. The success rate was remarkable. It was Irestone who first collected the data on what he described to be two distinct types of character disorders that he labeled the Slick and the Slob. In spite of Asklepieion's success, it was closed down after he left to work in juvenile corrections in Illinois. He died a tragic death in 1983 but his insights are the basic premise of this book. He had spent over 16 years of his life caught up in the penal system before he realized, "If I'm so smart, why am I here." He also concluded that two entirely different approaches must be made to "responsibilize" Slicks and Slobs. Even though he, an ex-Slick, hated the existing prison system in America with a passion, he recommended that Slicks be locked up to protect society, but his anger was directed at the fact that he and the corrections system, together, wasted hundreds of thousands of dollars and 16 years of his life without getting at the problem: The fact that Slicks and Slobs have abnormal thinking and reasoning processes and that they are oblivious to the fact they are different.

Slicks must be confronted with the reality that they are hung up on a perpetual destructive game of "I'm smarter than you" and "I'm going to make a fool out of you". Until he or she sees the game and decides to stop it, "responsibilization" will never take place.

Slicks use people to take shortcuts in life. They feel they can get what they want by outwitting everyone. Because they usually get what they want, they often get cocky and overconfident that they can pull off just about anything if they put their mind to it. They must be in control and when they lose control or are in a situation of being controlled, they react with rage. Anger is their driving force, anger at the rest of the world.

Mixing Slicks and Slobs is a disaster. Slicks are compelled to gain control and Slobs are easily impressed and controlled. A Slick will ruin any program if Slobs are around. Only a Slick can confront another Slick. It takes one to know one, or, in other words, you can't "B.S." the troops.

Any program for Slicks must be totally made up of Slicks and must be isolated from the rest of the world for a long period of time. Allowing a Slick to move in and out of the normal world will simply set the world up to be ripped off. That's why Slicks should never be put on probation. A Slick has the irresistable urge to play games with the system. Like putting a fox in charge of chickens, it just doesn't work.

The fundamental flaw in a Slick's viewpoint of the world is they feel it's a dog-eat-dog world where everyone else rips off each other and whoever is the smartest comes out on top, that it's all right to take advantage of another person as long as that person is stupid enough to let it happen. A sucker is born every minute and you're a fool not to take advantage of them. Slicks have contempt for the rest of the world. In their eyes, people get what they deserve. They justify their viewpoint by pointing out that there are crooked people all over the place. Politicians on the take, corporations that fix prices, judges who take bribes, policemen who commit burglaries, clergymen who steal from the congregation, Presidents who cover up burglaries. The newspapers are full of these stories every day and a Slick will point out with glee that it's all a matter of whether you get caught or not.

A Slick must be confronted with the fact that he's choosing to reinforce his position by seeing only that which confirms his viewpoint. That basically most people are honest, decent and good and the people he is pointing out are just some more Slicks—Slicks just like he is. There is a little Slick in all of us, just as there is a little Slob in all of us. When these character disorders become so serious that we cannot function normally, we have a problem. It's therefore necessary for Slicks to see good role models.

Slicks admire lawyers because lawyers have nothing to sell but their brains. To a Slick, a lawyer is smart enough to manipulate the system against the law-makers. Slicks giggle with glee when a lawyer finds a "loophole" to slide out a side door and foil the cops again. "All is fair in love and war" could only be the quote of a Slick. But like his other viewpoints, the Slick misjudges the legal profession also. A lawyer must have legal ethics and must work within the framework of these ethics or the lawyer will be disbarred and lose the privileges lawyers enjoy. Ethics, morality and legality are ignored by Slicks and have no place in their reasoning or conduct. Thus, Slicks must learn that one can be successful, clever and smart without being crooked, that one can find a legitimate place in the business and commercial world without cutting corners. A good salesman is a Slick, but a legitimate Slick. A good trial lawyer is a Slick, but an ethical Slick. Some preachers are Slicks but they are religious Slicks. Most politicians are Slicks, but honest Slicks.

Thus, being slick is not all bad, it's the American success story for many people, but what Slicks must learn is how to find the fine line between what is morally, legally and ethically right and wrong. Slicks must learn that if they continue functioning with their warped viewpoint they will live a life of anger behind bars.

Slicks do not empathize or feel any compassion for their victims. (I'm all right, you're not.) People are simply to be used. Therefore, Slicks must be confronted with the problems they've caused victims and restitution must be made. They must be exposed to the hurt and suffering they have imposed on others. Most Slicks rarely see their victims after the crime nor are they confronted firsthand with the emotional destruction they have caused. Face-to-face restitution is imperative. Slicks must learn to put themselves in another man's shoes or, as the Indians put it: "Walk in another man's moccasins."

Having a trusting relationship with another human being is not part of a Slick's makeup. They trust no one, (they feel everyone else is like they are, ready to rip you off if your guard is down).

They must learn that there are relationships that are mutual, giving and trusting doesn't have to hurt if everyone is honest.

Slicks are angry over not being given the respect they deserve (in their minds). They demand respect from others but give little respect in return. Slicks get respect by the force of fear. Like rattlesnakes, people respect them but sure as hell don't like them.

Living dangerously is a dominant part of a Slick's life. Crime and taking chances feed adrenalin into their veins. Slicks enjoy the "rush" of pulling it off. They must be shown that living dangerously and taking chances does not necessarily mean committing a crime. Mountain climbers, parachute jumpers and hang gliders get a rush too, but there are no victims except themselves if they are not careful.

Slicks routinely lie, con and manipulate as they shortcut their way through life. Every lie must be exposed; and every time they manipulate, they must be called on it and shown the game they are playing. Everything a Slick does must be cautiously examined with: "What's he up to now." It takes a Slick to deal with a Slick, therefore, any corrections worker must be at all times wary of being "put on" because a Slick will "run one by you" like breathing air.

In the Slick's world you don't give something without getting something in return. To them, all relationships must be rewarded with "what's in it for me?" Therefore, it is necessary for Slicks to give without getting anything in return. They must go out of their way to do good things for others with no conditions attached. Instead of trading stamps, they must give gold stamps, acts of spontaneous, benevolent love without a return except the happiness it brings. When Slicks have been "responsibilized" to this point, they can be slowly integrated back into society. Slicks must make the transition from total selfishness to sharing with others.

Once again, a book could be written on changing Slicks.* But without going into detail, a Slick must make the transition from being as predator who uses others to survive for another day, to an autonomous, self-supporting independent authentic person who

---

* Dr. Stanton E. Samenow has written an excellent book, *Inside the Criminal Mind,* Time Books, 1984, citing the work of Dr. Samuel Yochelson. The book is really about Slicks and the findings parallel the independent observations of Dale Irestone, cited in a previous source note herein.

survives by his own efforts without leaving a victim in the wake. To seek goals in appropriate ways through honest efforts, to "earn it the old-fashioned way", to care about others, the world, its environment and people instead of themselves and material things. To make the world a better place to live by putting something into it instead of ripping it off. To enjoy genuine accomplishments for themselves instead of phoney, self-deceiving triumphs based on making fools out of others.

A Slick can make it, but it's a long way. It demands a 180° turnabout in all their reasoning. But a Slob doesn't have to be a Slob and a Slick doesn't have to be a Slick, they both can be responsible, respectable people. But no judge is going to do it. No corrections worker can do it. They must do it for themselves. It's their problem and the most we can do is care.

THE DIFFERENCE BETWEEN SLICKS AND SLOBS

Slicks want to dominate the world, Slobs will gladly let them.
Slicks are leaders, Slobs are followers.
Slicks think they are smarter than everyone, Slobs think everyone is smarter than they are.
Slicks have pumped-up, arrogant self-esteem, Slobs have low self-esteem.
Slicks think they are OK, it's the world that's screwed up. Slobs think the world's OK but they're screwed up.
Slicks are over-confident, Slobs have no confidence at all.
Slicks will dare to try anything, Slobs will risk nothing.
Slicks play "kick you", Slobs play "kick me".
Slicks are loners, Slobs travel in packs.
Slicks think they need no one, Slobs need everyone.
Slicks get angry, Slobs get depressed.
Slicks think everyone is as bad as they are, Slobs think nobody is as bad as they are.
Slicks are rich drug wholesalers who get away with it. Slobs are

nickel and dime street dealers who get caught.

Slicks plan their crimes, Slobs blunder into them.

Slicks play "now I got you, you S.O.B." while Slobs play "now you got me, you S.O.B.".

Slicks take over prisons, Slobs get comfortable and let them.

Slicks are rarely caught and convicted, Slobs usually get caught and plead guilty.

Both are parasites and use other people to survive for another day.

Both are irresponsible and repeat their mistakes over and over.

Both fail to take charge of their lives or own their problems.

Both are losers but in different ways.

And both have the potential within them to change.

WHERE DO LITTLE SLICKS COME FROM?

Maybe they are born that way, but more likely they got started out on the wrong foot and simply got worse. Slicks were smarter in a conniving way than the rest of the kids on the block. Perhaps abused or mistreated, they soon grew to hate the dominating adults in their world. Perceiving the world to be inconsistent and unfair they soon discovered the power of manipulation and that they could make a fool out of just about anybody if they were quicker and smarter. They also found they could get away with an awful lot in this world without getting caught. Impatient about obtaining goals by legitimate appropriate means, they opted to shortcut everything. Soon they run their family rather than their family running them. Finding normal people's lives boring and mundane, they thrive on the excitement of crime. In the end, they enjoy the power of dominating other people and taking what they want.

It becomes an addiction difficult to break.

WHERE DO LITTLE SLOBS COME FROM?

Slobs come out of all kinds of homes. It has little to do with poverty, race, religion or opportunity. It is the stifling of a young mind by failing or not allowing a child to learn responsibility. Like a kid who never learns to swim, a little Slob never learns responsibility.

Chapter 9

THE LITTLE JIMMY STORY

Jimmy, a 12-year-old boy, was playing baseball in the front yard of his home one spring with a neighbor kid named Bobby.

Father came home early from work, parked the car in the driveway and proceeded toward the front door when he noticed the boys throwing the ball back and forth.

Father: Jimmy, I don't want you playing ball in the front yard. You're too close to the picture window. You could break it. Go over across the street and play in the park.

Jimmy: Yah, sure, dad, we'll do that.

Father went into the house, grabbed the evening newspaper, lit his pipe and settled down in his big easy chair when crash went the picture window.

He leaped from his chair, charged out the door in a rage, grabbed Jimmy by the back of his neck, raised him up in the air and gave him a swift kick.

Father: You dumb kid. I told you not to play ball in the front yard. Why did I ever get stuck with a stupid kid like you. You never listen, you meat-head.

With one swift motion, he dragged Jimmy into the house straight for Jimmy's bedroom where the boy was forthwith deposited. Slamming the door, father yells:

"You're grounded for the rest of the summer, you miserable little brat. And, furthermore, you're through with Little League. Anyone who can't throw the ball straight doesn't belong on any team."

Grabbing the telephone directory, father rifles thru the pages and finds glass repair and dials the number.

Father: (Speaking loud enough for Jimmy to hear.) "Hello, my fool kid just busted our picture window. I've got to have it fixed

right away...I know emergency calls cost more but if it doesn't get fixed, the flies, bats, mosquitoes and the rain...and God knows what else will be in our living room. Whatever it costs is going to come out of that kid's hide, I guarantee that."

Soon the glass repair company truck arrives and the crew installs a new picture window. They present father with a $250.00 bill. He reaches into his suit pocket and writes out a check for the full amount. "Darn kid," he grumbles.

The next morning Little Jimmy is sitting hang dog at the kitchen table, slowly stirring his oatmeal, when father sits down. At the appropriate time Father announces, "Remember we were going to go up north on vacation and rent that cabin on the lake? Well, we're not going. Stupo here, who broke the picture window, has just used up our vacation money, so we're staying home. You have him to blame, not me."

Now sister's angry, mother's angry and poor Jimmy is in the dog house. Incarcerated in his room, on strict probation, banished from Little League, Jimmy is doomed to spend a long, sad, dormant summer.

Let's suppose we start the story all over again right after the window is shattered, but this time mother hears the crash and runs to the front door.

Mother: What was that! My goodness, Jimmy broke the window. Oh, Jimmy, I hope you didn't get hurt. That glass was flying in all directions! Now, Henry, (looking at father), I'll take care of this. All you ever do is shout at that kid. She runs out and hugs Jimmy.

Mother: That's okay. You get home, Bobby. Everytime you play with Jimmy something like this always happens.

Father is standing in the doorway. Mother sees him there.

Mother: Now, don't get angry. Jimmy didn't mean for this to happen. It was an accident. Poor boy could have been hurt.

Father: That's all you ever do, no matter what that kid does, you stick up for him.

Mother: Henry, you know kids will be kids...poor Jimmy... Come with me, Jimmy, mother will take care of this.

So Jimmy and mother get into the car and drive downtown to the glass repair store. On the way Jimmy is crying.

Mother: Now don't feel bad, Jimmy, I know it was an accident. When I was your age I broke a window too. My father severely spanked me and locked me in my room. I never want to treat my child like that. We'll get a new window put in. It's no big deal. I've saved a couple hundred dollars out of the grocery money. We'll pay for it with that, but don't tell your father. He'd be furious.

So mother and Jimmy make arrangements with the glass repair company to install a new window. Mother pays for it in advance. They leave the store and proceed home.

Mother: Now don't feel so sad, Jimmy. It's just a stupid window. Hey, I know what we'll do! Let's stop at an ice cream shop. I see one just down the street.

And so that's how mother handles the problem.

Now, suppose we go back again and start all over again for the third time. Jimmy goofs up. The window is broken but this time a different kind of father responds, a father who was brought up to be responsible in a constructive way and is determined that his son will lead a responsible life also.

Father goes to the door and looks out at Jimmy.

Father: What happened, Jimmy?

Jim: The ball slipped and didn't go where I threw it.

Father: That makes me angry, Jimmy. I warned you that might happen. Now the window's broke. What are you going to do about it?

Jim: I'll fix it, dad.

Father: I didn't know you knew how to fix windows, Jim, but it's your problem.

Father returns to his chair, resumes reading the newspaper as Jimmy enters the living room and looks over the damage. He gets a broom and sweeps up the broken glass. The boy runs upstairs, comes down with an old sheet, takes a hammer and tacks up the sheet over the window. Father looks up over his newspaper.

Father: We used to be able to see the Smiths across the street. I don't think that's what you could call fixing the window.

Jim: I know, dad, I'm just trying to keep the flies and bugs out until I can figure what to do.

Father: Well, that makes sense, Jim.

Jim: Dad, how do you fix windows?

Father: Don't know, Jimmy, never broke one.

Jim: Are there people who fix windows for you?

Father: Don't know offhand.

Jim: Will you help me fix it?

Father: Nope. I didn't break it, not my problem.

Jim: Do you think the yellow pages will help me find somebody?

Father: It might.

Jim: What do I look under?

Father: Start with A and if you get to Z you probably missed it.

Jimmy thumbs through the book, one page at a time. After a few minutes he gets to G.

Jim: Hey, dad, it says "glass repair". Do you think they'll repair our window?

Father: You'll never know if you don't call them.

Jim: Will you call them for me?

Father: Not my problem. You didn't need me when you broke the window.

So Jimmy dials the number and gets an answer. He tells them the problem. After some discussion, Jimmy turns to his father.

Jim: Dad, what's credit?

Father: That's something you better learn about if you're going to break a lot of windows.

Jim: They want to talk to me about it.

Father: I suppose they do. They want to know how they are going to get paid.

Jim: Will you go down to the store with me?

Father: No, Jim, it's your problem. You have a bike, peddle on down and talk to them.

Jimmy gets on his bike and peddles away. About an hour later he returns with a troubled look on his face.

Jim: Dad, they want $250.00 to fix the window.

Father: I suppose they would. Sounds reasonable to me.

Jim: They said I could pay so much each week but I've only got $50.00 in my savings account from my paper route.

Father: You've got a problem. What are you going to do about it?

Jim: Well, I was thinking about earning some extra money. Will you pay me to mow the lawn every Saturday?

Father: Sure.

Jim: Will you pay me ten bucks each time?

Father: Nope. A neighbor kid knocked on the door the other night and said he'd do it for five bucks. That must be the going price.

Jim: Okay, I'll do it for that. Last winter you mentioned you wanted the garage painted. Will you pay me a hundred dollars to do it?

Father: Just a minute, Jim. Does that mean scraping the old paint off first? One coat or two coats? Who buys the paint?

They discuss the project, negotiate and make a deal. Jim gets hired to paint the garage. Jim goes back down to the glass repair company and hires them after agreeing to make monthly payments for the repair. The repair crew fixes the window. After they leave, father comes out, puts his arm on Jimmy's shoulder.

Father: Well, that was an expensive lesson to learn. You'll have to work most of the summer to make up for a moment of carelessness. But that's life and that's what responsibility is all about. I could have hollered at you and preached to you about responsibility but that would have been a waste of time. Responsibility is something you learn on your own and I'm proud of you. You were and are responsible. If you continue to own your problems and take charge of your life like you did this afternoon, I'll never worry about you when you grow up to be a man. You'll be all right. There are always going to be mistakes in your life but if you make it right, that's all that anyone can ask of you. By the way, we're going on vacation this summer at that cabin on the lake. I've got $250.00 in the bank, so let's get to work, son.

The story of Jimmy is perhaps simplistic but it does contain a bundle of psychology that can be broken down and it pretty much summarizes what this book is all about.

Let's analyze what happened in The Little Jimmy Story.

The First Parent (The Punishing Father).

1) A critical parent to child transaction. A dominating dictatorial parent coming down on a weaker, submitting child. Father is in total control. The boy takes what is dished out to him.

2) Negative punishment. The boy is banished to uselessness. Sitting in his bedroom and grounded to his house is a waste of time that stagnates the boy and doesn't allow him to grow. Little League, a positive part of his life is taken from him. Punishment for punishment's sake. Retaliation and revenge.

3) Parent took over the problem. The father calls, hires and pays for Jimmy's mistake, then takes it out on Jimmy by dumping a guilt trip on him.

4) Destruction of self-worth. The kid makes a mistake and father rubs his face in it by degrading and destroying the boy's self-worth.

5) No responsibility. The boy sits in his room and is not allowed

or given the opportunity to make up for his mistake.

In short, the first father represents the traditional criminal justice system in America. Property offenders are degraded and relegated to uselessness without an opportunity to be responsible for their crimes. Police officers, prosecutors, tough judges and prisons get caught up in this approach to corrections.

The Second Parent (The Rescuing Mother).

1) Nurturing Parent to Child transaction. A nurturing parent who rushes in to rescue the helpless child who is in trouble. Mother controls by warding off the tyrant and blames someone else (Bobby) and makes excuses for her son.

2) No consequences. The child gets himself in trouble and ends up getting an ice cream cone.

3) Parent takes over the problem. Rescuers who bail out children in trouble rob the child of the opportunity to be responsible. Responsibility is absorbed and transferred to the rescuer.

4) Child's self-worth is destroyed. The rescuing mother gets to feel good. "Now you'll love me more than your father!" But the child's self-worth remains stagnant.

5) The child experiences no responsibility. People who are bailed out of their trouble become dependent slobs and never learn responsibility.

In short, the second parent represents the opposite side of the punishing justice system. It feels sorry for and rescues wrongdoers. Probation officers, soft judges and defense attorneys get caught up in this approach to corrections.

The Third Parent.

1) An Adult to Adult transaction. The father treats the child in the same manner as he would treat an adult in similar circumstances. The child is given an opportunity to respond, to be responsible.

2) The problem becomes the punishment. Having to make it right becomes the only punishment necessary. The child must expend energy, put back that which has been destroyed.

3) Father refused to take over the problem. Even when the father knew the answers, he let the child find it out for himself. Responsibility is working one's way out of a jam, owning the problem and striving for a solution.

4) Self-worth is created. With responsibility comes self-worth. The father never degraded the child but was firm in putting the problem back on the person who had the problem.

5) The child experienced responsibility. Out of the three approaches to the problem, this approach was the only one that resulted in responsibility.

Briefly, the third parent is the only parent who does not create Slobs. If all parents cared about their children and made them responsible, there would be a lot fewer Slobs in this world and our criminal justice system could reduce its caseload tremendously.

The third parent should be the model for the justice system of tomorrow.

Some people may say that's fine, but what if Little Jimmy would have told his father to go to hell, that he doesn't fix any damn window for anybody or simply sits on his dead rear end and does nothing. The answer is simple. Remember Indian justice?

Father: That is a position you can take, Jimmy, but all we ask in this household is that we all be responsible for what we do. If you elect to be irresponsible and refuse to make it right, then you are not going to live among us. It won't be tolerated. I don't know what you will do. You may have to pitch a tent in the park and beg in the streets for food. If you steal, you'll be in trouble with the law, but that's your problem. If a bunch of social workers come after me for child neglect, then so be it. But I would rather be prosecuted and jailed than see my son grow up to be an irresponsible Slob who doesn't know how to stand on his own two feet. But the door will always be open, and as soon as you want to be responsible you will be welcome to live in this house. It's up to you.

And so it should be with our justice system of tomorrow. Be responsible, own your problems, take charge of your life and you are welcome to live among us. Refuse to be responsible and we will banish you to our jails and prisons. But the moment you choose to be responsible and show it, you are welcome back to live among us as a respected member of the community.

It's your problem...but it's our problem to care.

> "The worst sin towards our fellow creatures is not to hate them, but to be indifferent to them: that's the essence of inhumanity."
>
> -George Bernard Shaw-

AFTERWORD

There are so many forces working against the realization of an effective criminal justice system that change sometimes seems hopeless. There are self-serving interests that want to preserve things just the way they are. Then there are the sheer numbers of people caught up in the system and the immense amount of money that is being pumped daily into the system to make it survive for another day, another year; like a sick elephant that has sat down on its haunches and cannot move, we feed it meager hay and water to keep it barely alive.

There is a myth believed across America that justice equals conviction followed by imprisonment. This formula goes unchallenged, unquestioned.

In Reno, Nevada, there was established a restitution center to allow inmates from the state prison to be housed just prior to expiration of their prison terms. The idea was to allow the prisoners to work out of the restitution center and turn over their paychecks to the victims of their crimes. The concept was successful until one of the soon to be released offenders committed a rape. The powers that be reacted by closing down the restitution center. It apparently never occurred to them that people leave prisons every day and commit murder and rape, yet prisons are not closed down for the same reason.

There is a myth people believe, that offenders are sent off to prison to get better, to learn their lesson; and somehow they believe there are some magic people there, some Wizards of Oz in the form of psychiatrists, psychologists, social workers, counselors, etc., who get to people and change their ways. This is wishful thinking. The fact of the matter is most inmates get worse rather than better; and if they do leave prison and make it on the outside, there is always a psychological scar of anger that never goes away.

If our goal is revenge and retribution, then let's have the courage to say it. When Gary Gilmore was executed by a firing squad in Utah, there were numerous citizens who volunteered to bring their deer rifles down to the prison and do the job gratis.

The caveman Errg is alive and well in America today.

It is amazing how people will argue the merits and morality of capital punishment without questioning whether the courts and the jury system are capable of always convicting the guilty and never convicting the innocent. Those of us who work in the system do not have nearly the faith in the system as those who argue the cause of capital punishment. But these are deep and emotional issues that are not easily resolved.

What can be resolved is whether we want a criminal justice system that creates responsibility or one that takes away all responsibility, a system that creates self-sufficiency or perpetuates useless dependency, a system that puts something back into society or one that drains society of its productivity. The answer should be simple but we can't opt for responsibility, self-sufficiency and productivity and hold onto vengeance and retribution at the same time. They are inconsistent, diverse concepts.

In a free society, winners or losers are being produced in every family across the nation. That will go unchanged, but what we do with losers once they get caught up in the justice system can be changed. First of all, we must understand them and learn how they think. Then we must give them insight into their own behavior so they can change themselves. Judges and corrections officers must change their thinking and this will be difficult. It is easier for judges to respond with vengeance than understanding. With understanding there is always risk; with vengeance there is little or no risk. Judges who take chances with criminals take chances with their mortgaged home and job security next time they run for election. Tough, hard line judges risk very little at the polls and they know it.

Judges must either be specially and intensively trained in the psychology of character disorders so that they can give meaningful sentences or delegate this function to sentencing specialists. The latter alternative would appear to be the more desirable in that it would create corrections specialists who could devote full time to gaining insight into the criminal mind and thereby offer to the judges meaningful, constructive sentences.

Many probation officers who are now wasting their time writing reports and playing hide-and-go-seek with losers could find a challenging career as a sentencing specialist; this would become a respectable profession in its own right. But for this to come about, judges must have the courage to give up or share sentencing responsibility with the sentencing specialist. Judges who politically must answer to voters might find this hard to do.

Many, many years ago there was a man who was declared to be a criminal. He was tried, convicted and ordered to be executed. Before he died, he said many things that were recorded. It was a strange and revolutionary philosophy that greatly aggravated the Establishment. He said we should like and understand people who hurt us and take our property from us; that before we condemn others, we should take a good look at ourselves, and we shouldn't do to other people what we wouldn't want them to do to us. He said that when people harm us we shouldn't respond by harming them in retaliation but to respond with love, care, kindness and understanding. And, finally, he said that it is not an eye for an eye or a tooth for a tooth, but, rather, we must turn the other cheek.

The "Sermon on the Mount" falls on deaf ears. And it seems the citizens of our Bible Belt States who publicly expound their Christianity the most heed the "Sermon on the Mount" the least. It was Ghandi, a Hindu, who pointed out this inconsistency.

> "Ghandi, as I have mentioned, took a dim view of the Old Testament. He was offended by all the violence, the vindictiveness, the lust for revenge and punishment, the 'eye for an eye' of the Old Testament fathers and sometimes, it seemed to him, of the God they worshiped. But the New Testament he loved. 'Especially the Sermon on the Mount' he would say. 'It goes straight to my heart.' And he would sing out the words '...whosoever shall smite thee on the right cheek, turn to him the other also. That's what I've been trying to do, and to induce others to do all my life' he would say, "It is the basis of my creed of non-violence." "

It has often been said that a civilization is judged by how it treats the least of its members. There is a side to the collective American personality that cares, has compassion and has a desire to do something about the criminal justice system. This collective hope is to create a safer society where our children can grow up without the constant fear of crime and all it ugliness. And, there is the darker side of us that also reacts with anger, frustration, vengeance and meanness. The struggle between these forces will go on and on as history has clearly shown. The thousands who are caught up in our ever-expanding prison systems across our country will continue to spend useless, dependent lives simply because we don't understand the abnormal thinking and reasoning processes of their minds.

This senseless waste of money and human potential doesn't have to continue. We must act upon new insights and cast aside our myths and misconceptions. It's difficult to hear the soft voice of reason in the prevailing hurricane of hatred - but we must hear it.

ABOUT THE AUTHOR

"He is a breath of plain speaking from the Midwest, a puncturer of judicial myths and pomposity, a pioneer of common sense solutions to what ails the American criminal justice system.

Judge Dennis Challeen comes from Winona, Minn. (population 25,575) just down the road a piece from Goodview, Rollingstone and Homer. Yet this unlikely Mid-American setting has produced a bearded, burly bear of a man who is probably the leading authority on alternative sentencing in this country."

The John Marhsall Column
Seattle Post-Intelligencer
(4-1-83)

Judge Dennis Challeen has lectured extensively on criminal justice in over 100 cities in 32 states and 3 provinces of Canada. Feature articles and editorials about his concepts have appeared in numerous newspapers and magazines, including *Readers' Digest, Parade* and *US Magazine*. The judge has been the subject of TV documentaries and has been interviewed for national television on Tom Snyder's "Tomorrow Show", CBS "Evening News", "Christopher Closeup" and the "700 Club". He has authored three articles on criminal sentencing for national corrections magazines.

Judge Challeen, a part-time faculty member of the National Judicial College since 1978, has studied the criminal character disorder for more than 15 years. He stresses the concepts of confronting criminal offenders and juvenile delinquents with being responsible for their lives, to own their problems and that change must come from within. Using concepts of restitution, responsibility, Transactional Analysis, Reality Therapy and "old-fashioned make-it-right justice, he brings a totally new, yet old viewpoint that has been enthusiastically received wherever he has lectured.

Judge Challeen brings out a warm optimistic feeling that there is hope and there are constructive answers to common problems that face judges, legislators, probation officers, police, social workers, educators, parents, the business community and criminals who want to change.

The late Vice-President, Hubert H. Humphrey said that Judge Challeen's concepts "produce not only results but true justice."

In a society where one out of three young people will be involved in the criminal justice system before they reach the age of 18, his message is extremely important to concerned citizens everywhere.

BIBLIOGRAPHY

Berne, Eric. *Games People Play*. New York: Ballantine, 1978.
Glasser, William, M.D. *Reality Therapy*. New York: Harper & Row, 1975.
James, Muriel, and Jongward, Dorothy. *Born To Win*. New York: New American Library, Inc., 1978.

NOTES

Notes from Chapter 1
[1] Matt. 5:39
[2] Exodus, chapter 22
[3] The American Institute of Criminal Justice, 1315 Walnut St. Philadelphia, PA. *Just The Facts*, published by the American Foundation, Inc. 1978.
[4] id.
[5] id.
[6] id.
[7] From "Motel Holds County 'Guests' but Sheriff Holds The Key." *The Minneapolis Star and Tribune*, January 3, 1983.
[8] From the minutes of National Institute of Corrections, "Differential Incarceration Seminar", Lake Wales, FL, January 1980, p. 2.

Notes from Chapter 2
[1] Muriel James and Dorothy Jongward, *Born To Win* (New York: New American Library, Inc., 1978), 1-15.

Notes from Chapter 3
[1] Eric Berne, *Games People Play* (New York: Ballantine, 1978), p. 62. Dr. Eric Berne isolated many of the games people play and wrote a book on the subject. Dr. Berne established Transactional Analysis.

Notes from Chapter 6
[1] Authorized King James Version, (Nashville, TN: Gideons International 1973)

Notes from Afterword
[1] William L. Sherer, *Ghandi* (New York: Washington Square Press, 1979), p. 247.

INDEX

Apartheid, 8

Bible, 4

Common Law, 3
Conservatives, 43, 44, 49, 50, 52, 53
Costs
  of crime, 11, 65
  of incarceration, 11, 94, 117
Crime
  property, 10, 11, 131
  rate, 9, 10, 11
  violent, 5, 9, 10, 11, 18, 64, 98

Fronting, 3, 37

Judges
  education of, 7
  policies, 6, 76
  sentencing philosophies, 7, 8, 77, 79

Legislators, 9, 15, 77
Liberals, 43, 44, 49, 50, 52, 53, 109

Moses, 1, 2, 60, 62, 94
Myths, 5, 6, 8, 9, 10, 12

Native Americans, 62, 64
National Judicial College, 7

Old Testament, 2, 135

Parents, influence of, 21, 33, 107, 108, 122, 123, 127-132
Parole Boards, 8
Penitentiary, 4
Prisons, 5, 12, 59
Probation, 59, 89, 90, 91, 92, 93, 96, 116

Quakers, 4

Recidivism, 39
Restitution, 2, 59, 62, 64, 65, 66, 67, 68, 99

Sentencing, 6, 8, 9, 11, 12, 66, 77, 99
Suicide, 6

University of Nevada-Reno, 7

Victims, 2, 3, 12, 28, 64, 67, 97, 119

Making It Right by Dennis A. Challeen can be purchased directly from:

MELIUS & PETERSON PUBLISHING INC.
Suite 524, Citizens Building
P.O. Box 925
Aberdeen, SD 57402-0925
(605) 226-0488

Send $13.95 for the hardcover edition, $9.95 for the softcover. Please include $1.00 for shipping and handling. Visa and Mastercard accepted.

OTHER PUBLICATIONS BY
MELIUS & PETERSON PUBLISHING INC.

NATIONAL FOREST CAMPGROUND GUIDE
SOUTH DAKOTA RECREATION GUIDE
CLOUD PEAK PRIMITIVE AREA: TRAIL GUIDE, HISTORY
    AND PHOTO ODYSSEY
THE HEALTHIEST DINING IN AMERICA
AMERICA'S FAVORITES, NATURALLY
KIDS AND CARS; A PARENT'S SURVIVAL GUIDE FOR
    TRAVEL WITH CHILDREN
IT'S CATCHING: BASS FEVER; THE COMPLETE GUIDE
    TO BASS FISHING
MY NAME IS PATTY; A TEENAGER'S TRIUMPH OVER
    TRAGEDY

A catalog describing publications by Melius & Peterson Publications Inc. will be mailed on request.

Pq

PETTIGREW REGIONAL LIBRARY

PQ

345.05
C
Challeen
Making it right

JUL 2 9 2009

MAR 2 3 1987

PETTIGREW REGIONAL LIBRARY